The Bronx River

THE BRONX RIVER

AN ENVIRONMENTAL & SOCIAL HISTORY

MAARTEN DE KADT

Published by The History Press
Charleston, SC 29403
www.historypress.net

Front cover, top to bottom: See page 39 and page 91.
Back cover, clockwise from top left: See page 32; Main office of the West Farms Northern Union Gas Company in West Farms, the Bronx, discussed on pages 42 and 43. From North Side Board of Trade, The Great North Side of Borough of the Bronx, 1897, 102; See page 9.

First published 2011
Second Printing 2012

ISBN 978.1.60949.180.2

Library of Congress Cataloging-in-Publication Data
de Kadt, Maarten.
The Bronx River : an environmental and social history / Maarten de Kadt.
p. cm.
Includes bibliographical references and index.
ISBN 978-1-60949-180-2
1. Bronx (New York, N.Y.)--History. 2. Bronx River (N.Y.)--History. 3. Bronx River (N.Y.)--Environmental conditions. 4. Westchester County (N.Y.)--History. I. Title.
F128.68.B83K33 2011
974.7'275--dc23
2011017164

Contents

Preface: Introduction and a Framework for a Bronx River History 7

1. Production for Use: Minimal Impact 13
Before Contact with the Europeans 14
The Population Game 17

2. Producing a Surplus for Trade 19
Jonas Bronck and the First Settlers 20
Early Development of Water Power 23
The Richardson-DeLancey-Lydig Dam 25
The Manhattan Company: The First Benchmark, 1799 27

3. Industrial Production Develops 29
The Lorillard Dam: 1792 to the Present 31
Old Stone Mill, Tuckahoe: 1805 to the Present 33
Bronx River Paint Company, 1809 37
Bolton Bleachery: 1840s to 1930s 38
Other Milldams 40
Coal Gasification 42

4. A Place to Live 44
Railroads: Transportation Innovation Brings Pollution, 1841 44
Population Increase 46

Kensico Dam 49
Rivers Receive Waste: The Second Benchmark, 1896 52

5. Reclaiming the River 53
Pleasant Pursuits 54
Sewers 55
The Bronx River Parkway 58
Social Differentiation along the Bronx River 63

6. Another Cleanup 68
Bronx River Restoration Publishes the Third Benchmark 70
Bronx River Working Group 72

7. The Amazing Bronx River Cleanup 77
Bronx River Alliance 77
Five Parks 84
Westchester 100
Community Involvement 101

8. Reclaiming a Natural Resource 105
New Benchmarks: Good News, Bad News, Difficult News 106
Efforts to Reclaim the Bronx River and Its Watershed 110
The Bronx River 112

Epilogue 115
Acknowledgements 119
Appendix: Timeline 123
Glossary 127
Notes 129
Bibliography 145
Index 151
About the Author 157

Preface

Introduction and a Framework for a Bronx River History

The fire, which began at 5:18 a.m. on November 4, 2009, was under control by 7:50 a.m. Press reports said the 345,000-volt transformer fire at Yonkers Dunwoodie Substation caused no interruption of the delivery of electricity. But there was a problem that the press did not immediately report. A butterfly valve in the substation overflow containment area had failed, permitting fifteen thousand gallons of burning insulation oil to spill into a storm sewer, much of it traveling about a mile and a half to the Bronx River.[1]

Con Edison crews began the river cleanup almost immediately. They divided the affected portion of the river into five sections, from the most severely polluted to the less compromised parts of the river farther downstream. Con Ed had been in close communication with the state regulator, the New York State Department of Environmental Conservation. Not until later in that day did it become clear that the Bronx River Alliance, then an eight-year-old community organization, knew the river better than anyone and was able to offer indispensible cleanup advice.

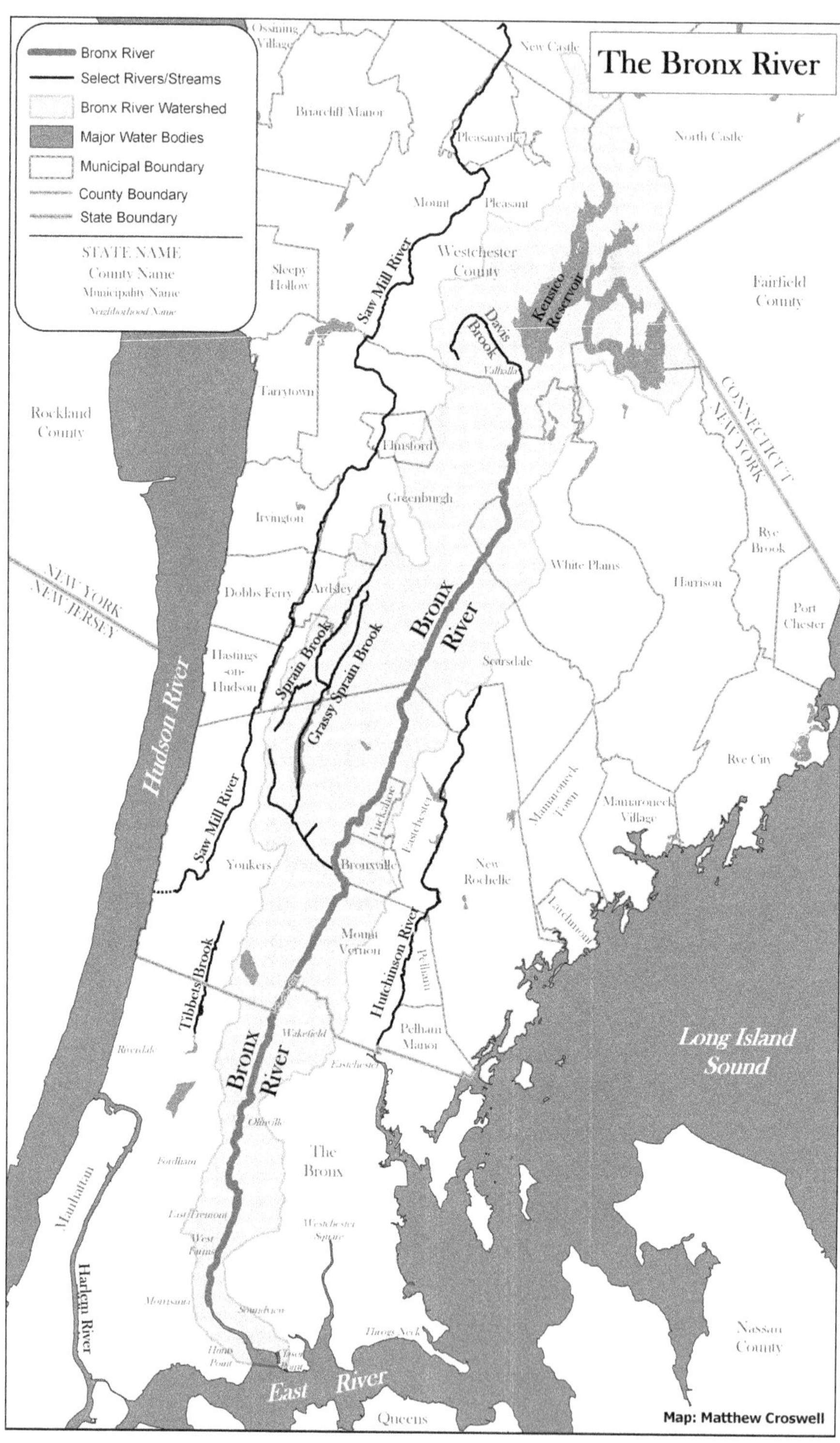
The Bronx River
Bronx River
Select Rivers/Streams
Bronx River Watershed
Major Water Bodies
Municipal Boundary
County Boundary
State Boundary
STATE NAME
County Name
Municipality Name
Neighborhood Name
Ossining Village
New Castle
Briarcliff Manor
Pleasantville
North Castle
Mount Pleasant
Westchester County
Sleepy Hollow
Saw Mill River
Davis Brook
Kensico Reservoir
Fairfield County
Valhalla
Tarrytown
Rockland County
Elmsford
CONNECTICUT
NEW YORK
Greenburgh
Irvington
Rye Brook
White Plains
Harrison
NEW YORK
NEW JERSEY
Dobbs Ferry
Ardsley
Bronx River
Port Chester
Hastings-on-Hudson
Sprain Brook
Grassy Sprain Brook
Scarsdale
Hudson River
Rye City
Mamaroneck Town
Mamaroneck Village
Saw Mill River
Tuckahoe
Eastchester
Yonkers
Bronxville
New Rochelle
Larchmont
Mount Vernon
Hutchinson River
Pelham
Tibbets Brook
Wakefield
Pelham Manor
Long Island Sound
Riverdale
Bronx River
Eastchester
Olinville
Fordham
The Bronx
Manhattan
East Tremont
Westchester Square
West Farms
Harlem River
Morrisania
Soundview
Throgs Neck
Nassau County
Hunts Point
Clason Point
East River
Queens
Map: Matthew Croswell

Above: At 290 feet above sea level, the Bronx River at its current headwaters comes out of a culvert under Legion Drive near Columbus Avenue and Broadway, Valhalla, New York. Streams and tributaries that contribute to the Bronx River include Davis Brook, also in Valhalla, and farther downstream, the Sprain Brook and the Grassy Sprain Brook. *Photo by Maarten de Kadt.*

Right: The Bronx River begins south of the Legion Drive Bridge, Valhalla, New York. The Bronx River Parkway is in the upper right-hand corner of the image. *Photo by Maarten de Kadt.*

In its current configuration, the twenty-three-mile river stretches from its source in Valhalla, New York's Westchester County to its East River mouth along the southern border of the Bronx. At Valhalla, the river is about 290 feet above sea level.[2] It is New York City's only freshwater river.[3] Europeans first began to use the Bronx River 372 years ago. The Bronx River has been a source of food and water, a boundary, a place of employment for freedmen and slave alike and a natural resource, used, despoiled and improved by people (both pre- and post-Columbian), businesses and government. Its rich history mirrors that of other urban rivers in the United States.

Over 400 years, communities around the Bronx River have dramatically changed in their racial and ethnic compositions and in size. Population and economic activity dramatically increased in the last 160 years, bringing riverbed alterations and water pollution. There have been many attempts to reclaim the river. Its environmental quality has been in constant flux.

Like so many other New Yorkers, Bronxites included, I had not heard of the Bronx River. My personal journey down the river started in 1997 when I began to teach social studies at Fannie Lou Hamer Freedom High School. My colleagues suggested that I teach something I was passionate about. I have always loved learning about New York City's history and had studied and taught that subject before. This seemed to be a perfect moment for me to learn more and to share what I knew with kids. Conveniently, the school is located in a historically rich neighborhood, about one mile south of the East Tremont section of the Cross Bronx Expressway. The construction of this section of the expressway is memorialized by Robert Caro in *The Power Broker*.[4] The students and I read about and walked through East Tremont.

Those walks introduced me to the Bronx River, and as a consequence, I learned about an organization involved in reclaiming the river, the Bronx River Restoration, whose staff was eager to teach teachers about water testing. I used my newly gained knowledge of water testing combined with a sense of the area's rich history to take students to visit the Bronx River. The students and I learned about the river's environment (the riparian environment), the local environment (the environment in watershed[5] communities) and the city's environment (broader environmental and social issues). I began to learn, with my students, about the Bronx River's history.[6]

This book reviews almost four hundred years of the river's history. In this section, I suggest a structural framework for examining Bronx River's environmental and economic history. Chapter 1 discusses the minimal adverse environmental effect of the use and abuse of resources by indigenous peoples before Europeans arrived. Chapter 2 discusses the initial claiming of land by newly arrived Europeans and the struggles those settlers faced in order to subsist, their use of waterpower, the transition to production of commodities beyond their own needs and the effects of these activities on the river's quality. Chapter 3 looks at the environmental effects of developing industry along the Bronx River. Chapter 4 examines the effects on the environment of increased population in Westchester County and the territory carved out of Westchester County to become "the Bronx." Chapter 5 looks at the Bronx River becoming part of the sanitary infrastructure for Westchester County and its spinoff, the Bronx, thus ending its possible use as a drinking water source. Chapters 6 and 7 examine the early and continuing attempts at restoring the river by newly formed organizations focusing on economic democracy, grass-roots organizing and community building, as well as on the environment. Chapter 8 ends by suggesting where we go from here.

Why tell the history of such a small river?

First, from an economic perspective, the Bronx River's history depicts the changing economic structure of its surrounding society. I have divided the Bronx River history into four distinct periods. The first three periods (subsistence through hunting, gathering and agriculture; mercantile trade; and industrial production) examine the relationship between changing forms of production and the pollution of the river. During the fourth period, I examine the continued pollution of the river, as production moved elsewhere but the population continued to grow.

These four periods help tell the environmental and economic history of the Bronx River. In each period, the adverse effects of economic production increase. But they do not occur in isolation. They are part of a complex amalgam of events. Any telling of history uses the constructs of historic periods to help render the flow of events understandable.

The disciplines of economics and history have influenced the categories chosen and the words selected in the telling of this history. My goal is to recount the history of the Bronx River that is simple to understand and that reflects the complexities of constant change, of both the human and the nonhuman environment.[7]

A second reason to tell the Bronx River story is that this river has suffered environmental damage that has been difficult—and sometimes impossible—to repair. A primary thesis of this work is that the taking back of our natural resources once degraded will be a difficult, long, slow, uphill, important task, requiring continual vigilance. A third lesson the history of this river demonstrates is that when the human community surrounding the river improves, so does the river. When the human community declines, the river is likely to decline as well. This is not a one-to-one relation. Change in one does not immediately lead to change in the other. But over time, change in one is reflected in change in the other. Finally, the history of the Bronx River tells a fourth story—a story of community organizing and involvement. People engaged in planning for change and who see that change implemented in things such as the design of a park become empowered to continue being civically engaged. Democratic participation is inspirational and a model that could serve other communities.

My hope is that the sum of all these parts teaches us more about the importance of preventing environmental degradation in the first place, that reclaiming our natural resources is essential to sustaining healthy communities and that while we face the powerful obstacles often placed in our way by business and government, we as individuals can effect change.

Chapter 1

Production for Use: Minimal Impact

Take a canoe trip down the Bronx River. Imagine what the river looked like before Jonas Bronck, the first European to settle near to it in 1639. The river flowed faster than it does today. It was not as straight. In fact, it meandered. The sounds were different then even as city and forest sounds are different today. The water quality was different: then you could drink it, today you should not. With the canopy of trees covering the river and hiding much of the nearby communities, a canoeist could easily imagine floating on this river before Columbus arrived. Those pre-Columbian times and the period of the early settling

While canoeing the Bronx River, it is easy to forget it is an urban experience. The sounds are urban but the view can take the mind far away in both space and time. *Photo by Bronx River Alliance.*

of the Americas by Europeans were periods of production for use—the first economic period examined in this book during which people inflicted minimal damage as a result of their use of the river and of the environment more generally.

BEFORE CONTACT WITH THE EUROPEANS

Land in the "Americas" was well used before the arrival of the European conquerors. Vibrant civilizations existed on the American continent prior to 1491. When the Pilgrims arrived, they found clearings in the forests and often-used pathways in woods. They encountered peoples with knowledge of the local terrain and the ability to provide food and shelter for themselves.[8] There is more than ample evidence that indigenous women were skilled in simultaneously growing corn, squash and beans. Their technique assisted in the control of weeds, did not erode the soil and provided healthy diets. Their methods helped replace nitrogen in the soil while producing foods with complete proteins.

> *Through production practices, women had a direct impact on the environment. Most eastern woodland traditions attributed to women the major roles in planting, weeding, harvesting, and distributing the corn, beans, squash, and pumpkins. Several varieties of each were planted. Corn was black, red, yellow, blue, and white, speckled and striped. Bush and pole beans were red, white, yellow, and blue. Cane and crooknecked squash and pumpkins appeared in several colors and varieties as well…Maize supplied zein, the protein in corn, but lacked lysine and tryptophan which were contributed by the beans. The synergistic effect of these amino acids resulted in a highly desirable protein combination.*[9]

Indigenous men hunted for food and fished. Gender roles often overlapped: "The sexes…played complementary roles in survival. But considerably more interaction and blurring of sex roles occurred than a strict sex-gender division of labor would imply."[10] Each season indigenous people moved from place to place to be near their food supply, to find seasonal firewood, to obtain shelter from winter weather and to move away from possible opponents.

There is ample evidence that indigenous peoples inhabited the mainland peninsula that came to be called the Bronx.

> *The land north of the Harlem River was occupied near the Hudson by the Manhattans and by the Weckquaesgeeks; eastward of them were the Siwanoys as far as Stamford in Connecticut—all branches of the Mohegans. This territory was usually spoken of as the mainland.*[11]

The mainland peninsula contained numerous freshwater waterways, each providing drinking water, food, transportation, waste removal and enjoyment. Aquehung is the name indigenous tribes gave to the river we now know as the Bronx River. Aquehung means a "fast stream flowing along high bluff." Indian sites existed near this and other nearby waterways such as the Sprain Brook, Davis Brook (both tributaries of the Bronx River), the Saw Mill River, the Hutchinson River and Tibbetts Brook. Two Indian sites existed near the mouth of Aquehung: one at what is now Clason's Point, another in Hunts Point.[12]

Indigenous peoples used Aquehung as a food source, a drinking water source, an obstacle, a border and a means of transportation. They built wigwams of bent-over saplings. Clay was used to fill the openings between branches. The mainstay of their diet was likely similar to the people of the Connecticut River who depended on salmon, shad, herring, bass and eel that "came up the Connecticut [River] by the hundreds of thousands." It was likely that they "derived about one-third of their annual food from the rivers."[13] We get an idea of the diet of the peoples in the valley of the Aquehung by comparing it to nearby peoples in southeastern New England. Perhaps 20 percent of their diet consisted of animal products (10 percent animal and bird carcasses, 9 percent fish and shellfish and 1 percent eggs). The remainder consisted of vegetable products (65 percent of the total was grain).[14]

An abundance of oysters found at the archaeological site in Clason's Point indicates that the Indians at the mouth of Aquehung likely ate shellfish. In 1848, Robert Bolton Jr. remarked, "The extensive '*shell banks*' on the shores of the East River, afford evidence that the aboriginal population must at one time have been very considerable."[15] Oyster consumption left long-lasting mounds of domestic refuse at a Clason's Point archaeological site that has been built over.[16] Because of the abundance of shellfish, it is likely that indigenous people living at the mouth of Aquehung ate more shellfish than the average New England indigenous person. Recent efforts to reestablish the oyster beds in that location make it clear that the currents at the mouth of the Bronx River provide a unique place well suited to shellfish.

The Clason's Point shell midden marked the site of a former settlement. While it appears that the inhabitants of that settlement placed their waste in a pile, it is possible that some waste may have found its way into water bodies or that some other portion may have been burned. Fires were also used to clear the land for agriculture, to chase animals in the direction of waiting hunters and to provide entertainment. The effects of fires were marked. For example, they enriched the soil. They reduced the amount of work that would have been necessary to fell trees.[17] But they also, at least temporarily, destroyed animal habitat and resulted in an ash runoff entering nearby water bodies.

Pre-Columbian people living along Aquehung were nomadic. They produced the food, clothing and housing they needed to subsist. Beyond those needs, there was no surplus. Subsistence is, of course, complex. It requires producing enough seed for the next year's planting while, at the same time, gathering enough food and fuel to make it through the winter and through the early postwinter months before food grew anew. Subsistence requires sufficient production for daily life and enough for the reproduction of the lives of the members of the group, clan, tribe or society.[18] While the process requires the coordinated activities of men and women of all ages, production for the use of the producer requires less output per person than more modern forms of production that focus on gaining profits by having workers make things for many other people.

The Population Game

Estimating how many people lived on the land before the Europeans arrived is difficult because of the annihilation of native populations by European germs and genocide. As many as 90 percent of the American native populations succumbed to disease.[19] Nevertheless, one estimate is

> *the total population of New England probably numbered somewhere between 70,000 and 100,000 people in 1600. (Lest this seem unimpressive, one should remember that the* English *population of New England was smaller than this even at the beginning of the eighteenth century, having reached only 93,000 people by 1700.)*[20]

Another estimate for the smaller territory of the lower Hudson Valley is more precise but may not be more accurate: in 1610, the Wappinger Confederation consisted of 13,200 people.[21] Other estimates for a different portion of the lower Hudson Valley admit their uncertainty:

> *We don't know for certain how many people lived in the communities on Mannahatta; estimates vary from three hundred to twelve hundred individuals, about the sidewalk population of one block on a busy afternoon in Midtown. Part of what complicates the estimation is that Mannahatta was probably not a year-round residence for most Lenape; rather, it was more of a three-season "resort." The Lenape moved to Manhattan for fishing in spring; stayed over to plant some crops, hunt, gather, and fish in the summer; then pull together their things in a furious fit of activity in the fall, bringing in the crops and smoking and drying the meat before the retreat to winter quarters.*[22]

There has been speculation that the Wappinger Confederation of eight tribes residing on the eastern banks of the Hudson at its tributaries comprised as few as five thousand people including the people on the lower Aquehung peninsula.[23] So, undoubtedly the number of people living in the Aquehung watershed was modest.

While there is no direct evidence that indigenous people used flowing streams as a place to dispose of their wastes, they may have done so. On the other hand, it is entirely possible that, for indigenous people, water was a sacred element and therefore no waste was intentionally released in it. However, *if* Native Americans used flowing water to wash away their wastes, two questions arise: what was the nature and composition of the wastes that may have been discarded into waterways, and what effect could those wastes have had on the waterways—did they cause degradation of the water's quality?

The answers seem easy. If wastes were deposited in waterways, they were organic and would have included debris from clearing land, animal carcasses, seasonal waste from establishing and reestablishing settlements, debris from seasonal fires and/or human excreta. As the human population was small by any count, this material could not have reached the water in large quantities, so they would have decomposed without adversely affecting water quality. Even the more problematic waste, debris from fire, would have been washed downstream. And it is unlikely that there would have been large quantities of materials even if the river was used as a primary waste disposal site. There simply was not sufficient waste to overpower the river's natural ability to cleanse itself. Therefore we can comfortably assume that when the Europeans arrived, Aquehung water quality was virtually pristine. With the arrival of Europeans and their patterns of mercantilism, and later industrialization and substantial increases in population, this river loading changed, as did the way in which social and economic production and reproduction occurred. With the arrival of Europeans, production increased to create a surplus to be sold for profit. The increase in production and later in population, over time, had its own degrading effect on Aquehung's water quality.

Chapter 2

Producing a Surplus for Trade

European farming techniques were different than those of Native Americans.

> *The elements of the* [European and Native American]...*systems* [of agriculture] *differed at the level of production in their extractive technologies (hoe versus plow, fire versus saw, arrow versus gun), production of subsistence (shifting versus settled agriculture, hunting versus animal husbandry), and gender relations of production (females versus males in the field). But in addition to subsistence, colonial production was also oriented toward mercantile trade in the international market, causing added ecological stress.*[24]

With the establishment of industry, the clash of technologies and of social relations had a profound effect on the environment of the Aquehung Valley. In addition, the expanding population increased the production of waste that in later periods had serious harmful effects. In this early mercantile period (the mercantile period is the second economic period examined in this book), however, relatively small quantities of organic waste were easily processed by the environment. For these early settlers, the river's water remained good enough to drink.

JONAS BRONCK AND THE FIRST SETTLERS

In 1609, when Henry Hudson opened the door to the European settlement of New York, the indigenous peoples who had long lived there had no conception of landownership.

> *Private ownership of land and the hierarchical relations of domination and exploitation familiar in Europe were unknown to the Lenape... By custom and negotiation with its neighbors, each Lenape band had a "right" to hunt, fish, and plant within certain territorial limits.*[25]

Tribal peoples before the Europeans arrived saw their relationship to the land as limited to its "use." They had no concept of "owning" it and thus did not understand the concept of "selling" land. Ownership, as described in a written document we call a "deed," was a European construct.

> *When it came time to transfer property rights, those deeds allowed the alienation of land as a commodity, an action with important ecological consequences. To the abstraction of legal boundaries was added the abstraction of price, a measurement of property's value assessed on a unitary scale. More than anything else, it was a treatment of land and property as commodities traded at market that distinguished English conceptions of ownership from Indian ones.*[26]

What followed is a history of ownership, domination and displacement by Europeans.

Among the first to arrive in Nieuw Amsterdam's northern frontier was Jonas Bronck. He arrived in 1639, fifteen years after the Dutch established their colony on the lower-most tip of Manhattan. Bronck was a Swede who obtained his farm under the auspices of the Dutch West India Company.

> *On August 3, 1639, there was conveyed by the Indian sachems, Tequeemet, Rechgawac, and Pachimines, to the West India Company, through Secretary Cornelis Van Tienhoven, a tract of land...The boundaries of this tract, especially to the northward, are rather indefinite; but the tract*

> *later became the lower portion of Westchester County, and later still, the Borough. The transfer was made "in consideration of a certain lot of merchandise," which the sachems acknowledged to have received.*[27]

Bronck worked his farm with his wife and a number of indentured servants. He was one of the non-Dutch nationals whose "presence didn't, in the long run, augur well for the company's ability to preserve Nieuw Netherland as a Dutch colony."[28]

Bronck and his family settled on a five-hundred-acre farm on the banks of a river in the area of the Bronx now known as Morrisania.[29] Bronck's farm may have stretched as far north to what is now 182nd Street. "There is speculation that Jonas Bronck erected a mill and laid out a plantation… on the Bronx River at what is now the southern end of Bronx Park."[30] Whether Bronck erected the mill or whether his farm stretched that far north, by the 1680s there was a mill on the 182nd Street location.

The following postmortem comments about Bronck give some insight into his lifestyle:

> *His estate was administrated by friends in Harlem, New York…From the inventory of his estate, we must believe that Heer Bronk* [sic] *was a gentleman of education, culture, and refinement; for there appear books, silver table service, linen napkins and "six linen shirts." The books were chiefly of a religious or theological character, polemical discussions so dear to the reader and writer of that day, and were in several languages; so that Heer Bronk* [sic] *must have been something of a linguist. His son Peter afterwards settled near Albany, in whose neighborhood, so it is said, his descendants are to this day.*[31]

Peter Bronck[32] may have been a cousin or uncle. The relationship to Jonas is unclear. Still standing in Coxsackie, near Albany, New York, on the western side of the Hudson River, is the original house Peter Bronck built. That house provides a visual impression of the kind of house Jonas may have built on his farm quite a bit farther to the south.[33] Recent scholarship tells us that, in 1643, Jonas died of natural causes only four years after he arrived.[34] That he died peacefully does not mean that he lived in peace. Anne Hutchinson (of Hutchinson River Parkway fame), who farmed not

Left: Today Peter Bronck's house is part of the Green County Historical Society Museum in Coxsakie, New York. Jonas Bronck's house, which no longer exists, may have been similar. *Photo by Maarten de Kadt.*

Below: Looking back from 1912, the year Stephen Jenkins published his history, to the period in which the Dutch controlled Nieuw Amsterdam and the mainland territory north of the growing city. *Stephen Jenkins's* The Story of the Bronx: From the Purchase Made by the Dutch from the Indians in 1639 to the Present Day.

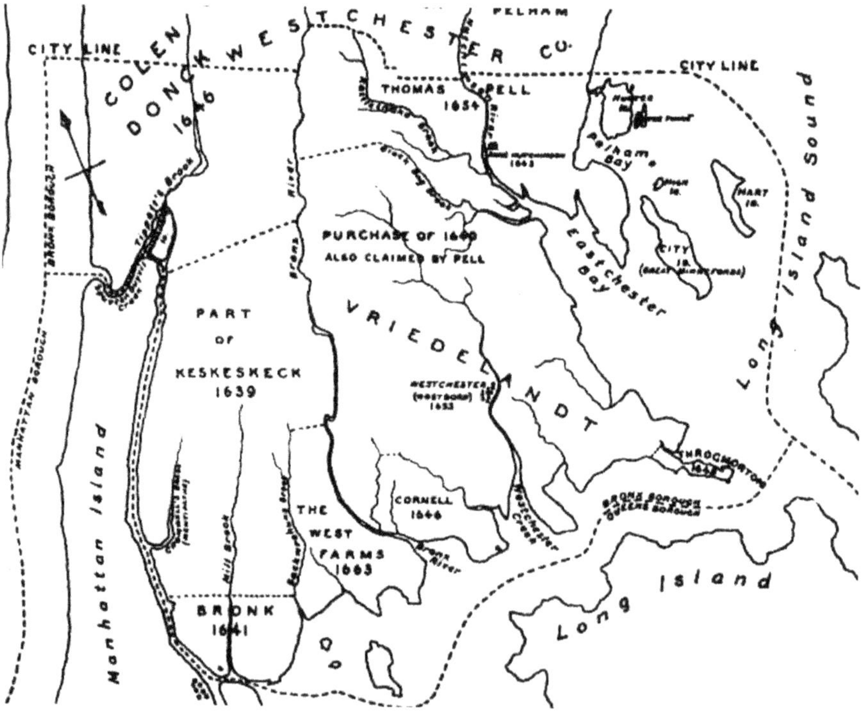

too far to the east of Broncksland, was killed in a confrontation with local Indians in 1643, followed soon thereafter by the destruction of the home and barns of John Throckmorton's (of Throggs Neck fame) by the same group of Indians, although the Throckmortons managed to escape.[35] Those were also years of conflict between the Dutch and Indians, the most famous of which was Kieft's War that lasted from 1643 to 1645. Wars and mercantile conflicts between the Dutch and English were also plentiful, thus further heightening tensions in Nieuw Netherland.

While Bronck's stay in Nieuw Netherland may have been short lived, his legacy is long, as exemplified by the use of his name to identify the river bordering his farm. Aquehung became known as Bronck's River, later renamed the Bronx River.[36] The native peoples used a descriptive term, while the Europeans named the river after a person. This change of name is emblematic of a change in the attitude toward land and water use and ownership brought by the Europeans. Now property could be treated as a commodity.

Early Development of Water Power

Mills on various waterways provided an important source of power and wealth to early European settlers throughout New England. Mill owners struggled over the control of the kinetic power water provided them on the 110-mile-long Merrimack River in Massachusetts and New Hampshire, where downstream millponds encroached on the waterpower available to the nearest upstream mill.[37] The mill owners on the Bronx River, whose ponds were sufficiently dispersed, did not seem to have this problem. While there were mills on the 410-mile Connecticut River,[38] that river does not present the same issues, as the hardly navigable, much smaller Bronx River, although it too became polluted. The 19-mile Woonasquetucket River in Rhode Island was also known for its mills (eighteen as opposed to the twelve Bronx River mills). Just as on the Bronx River, the Woonasquetucket River today supports an active community working to reclaim a waterway damaged by years of industrialization and neglect.[39]

There were tidal mills constructed on New York waterways as early as 1666. Thomas Haddon's inheritance of a sawmill on the Hutchinson

River occurred in 1725. Clearly, the Saw Mill River, in what is now Yonkers, received its name from its use as a power source. And Jacobus van Cortlandt dammed Tippetts Brook (named after the man who first built a mill at the site, George Tippett) as early as 1700 for a grist- and sawmill that operated until 1902. The continued existence of Van Cortlandt Lake, in the 1,122-acre park with that name, still depends on this dam.[40]

Descriptions of water mill technology abound. Movement is transmitted to the machinery by the power of moving water. Using the jargon of mill wheels, in an undershot wheel, the power of the flowing water turns the mill while a breast wheel uses the power of falling water. Milldams cause silting. They restrict the passage of migratory fish, and they restrict the river's flow. No description of Bronx River milldams tells us how wastes from the manufacturing processes, or from the ordinary lives of the workers and the mill owners, were managed. In each case the river was conveniently available for the discard of wastes.

The earliest mills assisted local farmers in preparing lumber and grinding grain, much of which they used themselves, though surpluses were occasionally produced for sale at the nearby local market, New York City. When New York wanted to strengthen its fort, timber, fashioned into stockades, came from Westchester. Increasingly, timber was cut for such commercial purposes.[41] Early colonists have been described as practicing "subsistence agriculture."[42] They produced what they needed. They milled and ground what they needed. When surpluses were produced, or when they were demanded, they could be shipped to the nearby city and sold. The money received was used to buy other products. Mill owners realized they could gain profits by producing more than they needed for their own use or the use of their local communities. They began to increase the production of their commodities and sell them on distant markets with the hope of gaining even more profits: "The colony was still a colony of traders...From the slave to the colonist, from the colonist to the patron, from the patron to the director, and even from the director to the company, there was little besides struggling for pecuniary advantage."[43] As more timber was cut and grain was grown, mill owners who processed and sold these materials prospered.

The Richardson-DeLancey-Lydig Dam

Functioning milldams on the Bronx River span a 145-year period. The Richardson Mill Dam was the first milldam on the Bronx River. It was primarily a grist- and sawmill. Thus it processed only organic materials that, in those early days, the river had ample capacity to absorb. The families that operated this mill employed both freemen and slaves. Whatever waste these folks produced and deposited into the river were likely also absorbed by the river.

The dam, located at about 182st Street, still exists. It was probably built toward the end of the seventeenth century: "Upon the 16th of August, 1680, the town of Westchester did give and grant unto William Richardson and his associates, the privilege of the stream of Bronck's river, to set up *two mills*, viz:—One saw and a corn mill."[44]

Over time, the Richardson Mill became the property of Peter DeLancey. In addition to being part of the Bronx River story, this mill played a role in the Revolutionary War. During that war, the Bronx was part of a territory then called Westchester County. It was a no man's land in which colonialists and Loyalists skirmished with each other. When the Bronx River flooded, it inhibited the east-west movement of troops. The mainland peninsula and the Bronx River Valley provided an escape route for George Washington after his army was defeated in Brooklyn in August 1776. The defeated army crossed the East River at Kips Bay, moved up Manhattan and then through what is now the Bronx to White Plains. In October 1776, the successful Battle of White Plains enabled Washington's army to survive, regroup and continue fighting this long, punishing, seven-year war. The territorial back and forth between Loyalists and colonialists in Westchester continued throughout most of the Revolutionary War. Properties were destroyed and hills were named. Gun Hill, named after the gun placements near to its summit, in what is now Woodlawn Cemetery abutting the Bronx River, is a good example. Surely the water bodies impeding troop movements received a great deal of debris, as they would during any war.

Colonel James DeLancey, son of "Peter of the Mills," commanded the Westchester Light Horse supporting the Loyalist side of this war. During the winter of 1778–79, Colonel Aaron Burr and his men overpowered

The DeLancey Mill Dam is depicted on the left. The mill works are on the eastern shore of the Bronx River overlooked by the DeLancey mansion. This bucolic scene disguises the harsh reality that the DeLanceys used slaves to operate their mill works. *Robert Bolton Jr.'s* History of the County of Westchester from Its First Settlement to the Present Time, *vol. 2.*

The DeLancey Mill is long gone, but its dam serves as the primary feature of a public park on the west bank of the river. Waders in the Bronx River are assisting canoes in an annual river festival, the Amazing Bronx River Flotilla. A closed-to-the-public section of the Bronx Zoo occupies the dam's east end. *Photo by Maarten de Kadt.*

a blockhouse that commanded the crossing of the Bronx River at the DeLancey Mill. When the Loyalists eventually lost the war, DeLancey's Mill was confiscated. Ownership of the mill was transferred to Phillip Lydig. Henceforth, the mill became known as the Lydig Mill until Bronx Park was formed in 1888.[45]

Even though the river may have been degraded during the war, silted by the dams and despoiled by mill and human wastes, nature has a wonderful way of restoring itself if not too greatly overpowered. The river was able to recuperate from these incursions.

THE MANHATTAN COMPANY: THE FIRST BENCHMARK, 1799

By the end of the 1700s, a report produced for Aaron Burr's Manhattan Company set a high benchmark of Bronx River water quality. The 1790s was a period of financial innovation. The New York Stock Market was formed, several marine insurance companies were established and, in 1799, Aaron Burr formed the Manhattan Company, predecessor to Chase Bank, supposedly as a canal and water company. These early financial corporations were early harbingers of industrial capitalism. At that time, New York City was confined to the southern part of Manhattan Island. The city required, as the next half century demonstrated, an abundant supply of safe drinking water, as well as water to put out dangerous fires among densely placed wooden structures. The Manhattan Company was asked to evaluate whether the Bronx River could assist in supplying water to the increasingly thirsty New York City.

In 1799, engineer William Weston, with some equivocation, documented the suitability of the Bronx River as a drinking water source to the city's Common Council.

> *From the representations made respecting the water of the Bronx, I believe many persons will have hastily concluded that it was unfit for use. When it is considered that the principal cities in Europe, are necessarily supplied from Rivers, and with water, generally taken from those parts, which from a variety of causes, are most impure, and yet*

> *at the experience of the ages has not evidenced any known ill effects, arising from the practice, I conceive that little fears will be entertained of the salubrity* [sic] *of the water of the Bronx—which is a collection of innumerable Springs, issuing from a rocky and gravelly country, and running with a rapid current, over a bed of the same materials. It will be conveyed into the city without any additional impurity, and e're it is distributed from the Reservoir, it will by a mode of purification hereafter described, then rendered as clear as Spring Water.*[46]

With the river's environmental quality established, New York State conferred a charter on the Manhattan Company to convey water to the city. Because Burr and the other principals of that firm were more interested in finance than in water, the Manhattan Company took no action to build the required aqueducts that could transport Bronx River water to the south.[47] In 1821, the mayor once more looked to the Bronx River as a potential domestic water source, but again no action was taken. Even though plans were already underway to obtain water from another source—the Croton River in Westchester County—the delays in obtaining clean drinking water played a role in the 1832 cholera epidemic and a catastrophic fire in 1835. The Bronx River remained untapped as a water source for New York City at that time. However, the 1799 report to the Common Council tells us that no matter how the Bronx River had been used prior to that date, its water quality was good enough to drink. That would change in the century to follow.

Chapter 3

Industrial Production Develops

The Bronx River's swift-flowing water proved an ideal source of power. Twelve or so mills used the Bronx River as a source of power for subsistence, mercantile and industrial production and for transport, with the first mill beginning operation during the 1680s and the last mill operating as late as 1934.[48] Dams harnessed the river's power while at the same time impeded the ability of anadromous fish[49]—like alewives—to spawn upstream. The operation of mills, however, decreased the quality of the water in the same ways as mills on other rivers did. During the industrial period (the third economic period discussed in this chapter), the production of commodities produced primarily with the explicit intention of selling them for profit, took hold. Beginning in 1841, railroads further used and abused the river's water.

As industrialization expanded, the water's power was used in the production of commodities such as tobacco (snuff), paint, cotton and cloth, rubber products and gun powder, in addition to grinding grain and cutting wood for growers and harvesters. While the 1800s saw the greatest increase of production using the river's power, by the end of the 1800s, the dependence on water as a source of industrial power diminished. The river was still used to flush away wastes and provide water for industrial processing of rubber and coal gas. It was not until the nineteenth century that industry on the Bronx River caused real long-term damage to the river's environment.

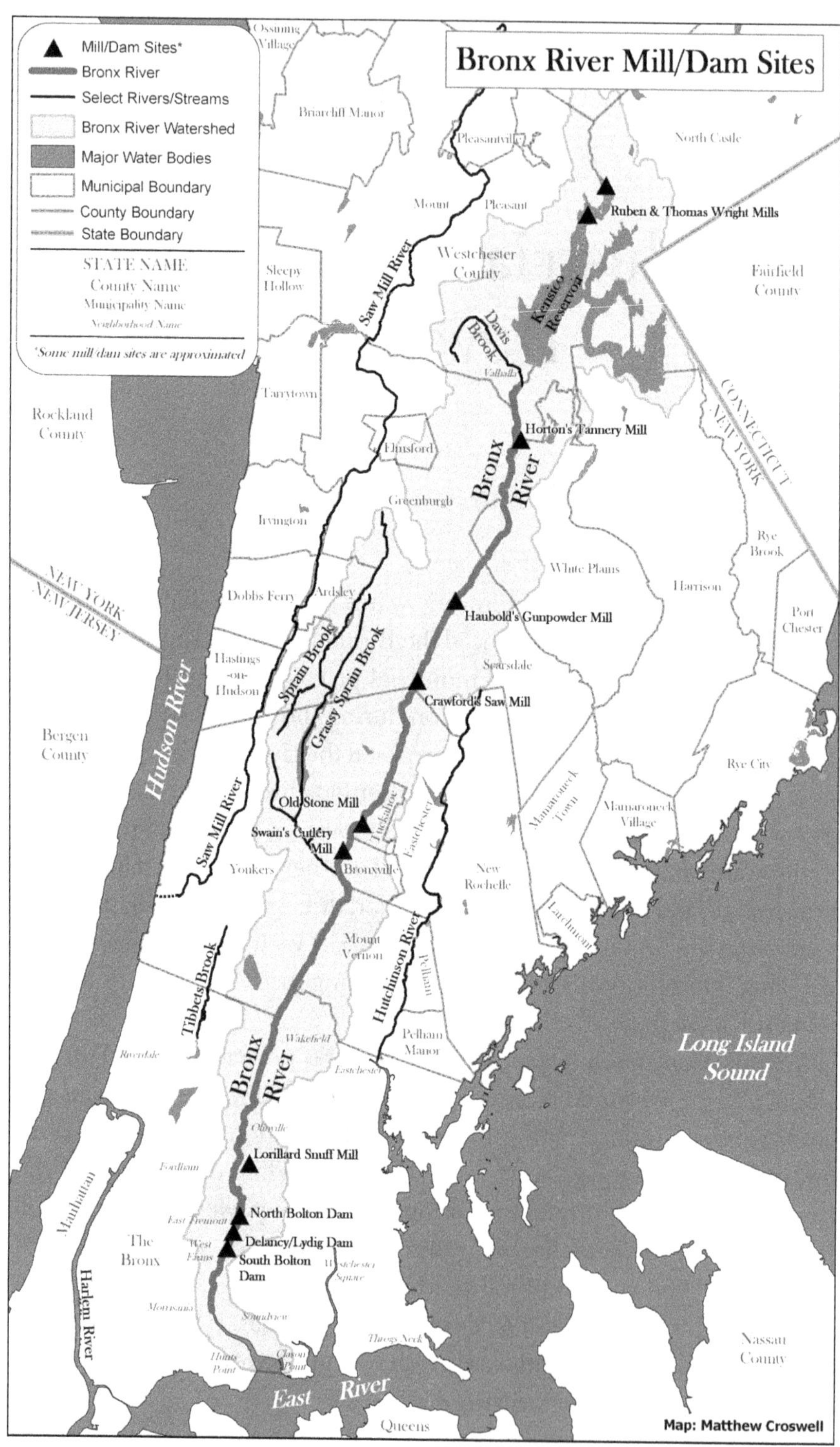
Bronx River Mill/Dam Sites
Mill/Dam Sites*
Bronx River
Select Rivers/Streams
Bronx River Watershed
Major Water Bodies
Municipal Boundary
County Boundary
State Boundary
STATE NAME
County Name
Municipality Name
Neighborhood Name
*Some mill/dam sites are approximated
Ruben & Thomas Wright Mills
Horton's Tannery Mill
Haubold's Gunpowder Mill
Crawford's Saw Mill
Old Stone Mill
Swain's Cutlery Mill
Lorillard Snuff Mill
North Bolton Dam
Delancy/Lydig Dam
South Bolton Dam
Kensico Reservoir
Davis Brook
Saw Mill River
Bronx River
Sprain Brook
Grassy Sprain Brook
Hudson River
Tibbets Brook
Hutchinson River
Harlem River
East River
Long Island Sound
Westchester County
Fairfield County
Rockland County
Bergen County
Nassau County
CONNECTICUT
NEW YORK
NEW JERSEY
North Castle
Briarcliff Manor
Pleasantville
Mount Pleasant
Sleepy Hollow
Tarrytown
Elmsford
Greenburgh
Irvington
Dobbs Ferry
Ardsley
Hastings -on- Hudson
White Plains
Harrison
Rye Brook
Port Chester
Scarsdale
Rye City
Mamaroneck Town
Mamaroneck Village
Tuckahoe
Eastchester
Bronxville
Yonkers
New Rochelle
Larchmont
Mount Vernon
Pelham
Pelham Manor
Valhalla
Wakefield
Eastchester
Riverdale
Olinville
Fordham
East Tremont
West Farms
Westchester Square
Morrisania
Soundview
Throgs Neck
Hunts Point
Clason Point
Manhattan
The Bronx
Queens
Map: Matthew Croswell

The Lorillard Dam: 1792 to the Present

The first industrial mill on the Bronx River produced snuff, a finely ground tobacco product sometimes scented with an oil or a perfume. Pierre Lorillard established P. Lorillard Company, later known as the Lorillard Tobacco Company, in New York City in 1760. The Bronx River mill, to which the company moved in 1792, used rose petals to scent their product.

After Pierre died, the company passed into the hands of his wife and eventually his sons, Peter and George. The Lorillard Snuff Mill replaced a previously existing wooden gristmill owned by Richard and Mary Hunt. The Lorillard Tobacco Company replaced the wooden mill with a fieldstone and brick mill in the 1840s. That building still stands today newly renovated as the Lillian and Amy Goldman Stone Mill in the New York Botanical Garden. The millworks have not been restored, but its history is recorded: "The millstones used in the grinding were powered by two wheels, about 15 feet in diameter, in the basement. These were turned by sluices of water channeled into the building."[50]

By 1912, the Lorillard Snuff Mill in the New York Botanical Garden was no longer used as a factory. It had become a storage space. *Stephen Jenkins's* The Story of the Bronx: From the Purchase Made by the Dutch from the Indians in 1639 to the Present Day.

Bronx River enthusiasts in 2002 carry their canoes around the Lorillard Snuff Mill. *Photo by Maarten de Kadt.*

The Lorillard Dam, located in the New York Botanical Garden *Photo by Maarten de Kadt.*

In 1870, the company moved the business to New Jersey. The Lorillard Bronx River estate, along with the mill, was purchased by New York City in 1884. In 1888, the property became part of Bronx Park. The mill was variously used as storage, a carpentry shop, as a police headquarters or merely left vacant. Water was no longer used to power its machinery. Today the New York Botanical Garden uses the "oldest extant tobacco factory,"[51] the Old Snuff Mill, as a restaurant for the general public and for special events, as well as for offices.[52]

Old Stone Mill, Tuckahoe: 1805 to the Present

Built around 1805, a wooden mill in Tuckahoe started as one of the nation's earliest cotton mills.[53] The Old Stone Mill may have been erected ten years later in 1814 after the wooden structure burned down. The cotton thread–producing enterprise was called the Eastchester Manufacturing Company. At that time, an abundance of cotton reached the market as a result of Eli Whitney's cotton gin, which was invented in the late 1790s. Even so, this mill competed with a Pawtucket, Rhode Island mill built in 1793 and other New England mills, such as those on the Woonasquetucket River, also in Rhode Island. After 1821 when construction began, the Lowell Massachusetts mills integrated the production of cotton products in newly designed, water-powered factories. They combined production of thread, cloth and the use of labor, mostly young women, as factory workers. The price of cotton products fell, thus providing the small Westchester mill, and all the other single product cotton mills, with serious additional competition.

During the War of 1812 between Great Britain and the United States, while the Old Stone Mill was in its heyday as a thread manufacturer, it produced thread used in garments for soldiers. Beginning in 1821, financial difficulties led to foreclosure and changes in ownership of the mill. Ownership again changed hands under further financial pressure in 1841. The property on which the Old Stone Mill stood decreased from seventy-six acres to forty-five acres by 1849. By the early 1850s, the enterprise was renamed to the Tuckahoe Cotton Factory. In 1853, "William J. Tait and his older sister, Elizabeth Ann Carpenter, sold the mill property to the Hodgman Rubber Company for a sum of ten thousand dollars."[54]

At that time, the Old Stone Mill started manufacturing rubber products. Lasting for nearly three quarters of a century, it produced rubber products for two wars: the Civil War and World War I. The firm employed six to seven hundred employees at the Old Stone Mill and at a number of nearby locations.[55] At some point the mill owners stopped using the strength of the river's flowing water for power. By 1913, photographs showing smoke coming out of tall stacks imply that steam had become the mill's power source.[56] The steam was probably produced using water taken from the river. In 1928, a British American pharmaceutical company, Burroughs-Wellcome Pharmaceuticals, purchased the factory site. After that company moved, the mill building remained unused until 2002.

Cotton used for the thread first manufactured in the mill was an organic material. If the cotton-spinning process dumped wastes into the river in relatively small quantities, they would have degraded. Amounts dumped beyond the river's natural ability to absorb the waste would have been more serious, causing eyesores or obstructions. The chemicals used to bleach and dye cotton would have caused the river serious harm. Workers also created their own wastes—food waste and excreta, both organic. The river cannot absorb more than a certain amount of organic waste, and small amounts of chemical waste would have been diluted. In its early days, the Old Stone Mill is unlikely to have exceeded those thresholds.

Rubber production, which came later in the mill's history, presented a more serious problem. Its manufacturing process required the introduction of more chemicals than did cotton production. Wastes produced were probably deposited into the flowing river that also provided power to the plant. Those wastes contributed to the overall loading and degrading of the Bronx River.

The old mill building remained neglected until August 1992, when, as a result of the actions of local community groups and their elected officials, it gained landmark status. Reminiscent of the Lorillard Snuff Mill farther downstream, the mill stood vacant for a number of years, after which it was transformed into a restaurant in 2002. Within that restaurant is a display of historical photographs and plaques depicting

The Tuckahoe Old Stone Mill in its life as a rubber manufacturing plant circa 1914. *Courtesy of the Tuckahoe Historical Society.*

This image of the Old Stone Mill, circa 1860, is on display inside the Old Stone Mill Restaurant in Tuckahoe, New York. *Courtesy of the Tuckahoe Historical Society.*

The Old Stone Mill on the Bronx River Channel in Tuckahoe, New York, in August 2010. *Photo by Maarten de Kadt.*

In 2002, the vacant Old Stone Mill was transformed into a restaurant. Tuckahoe, New York, August 2010. *Photo by Maarten de Kadt.*

the mill's history. One summarizes the history very briefly: "In 1821 the mill began to experience difficulties and eventually failed. It was sold in 1852 to Hodgmen Ruber Co, and converted to the manufacture of rubber goods. Their products were of the finest quality and during WWI they equipped the army with their excellent rubber raincoats."

This pleasant restaurant setting with its historical memorabilia strengthens the river's current role as a place of recreation and relaxation.

Bronx River Paint Company, 1809

An early mill likely to have caused damage to the Bronx River was farther downstream: the Bronx River Paint Company. Incorporated in 1809,[57] its paint-making process used pigments, including lead. Those materials likely escaped into the Bronx River, and as they do not degrade, they surely caused some damage—lead bioaccumulates[58] in the food chain. This company is mentioned in the Laws of the State of New York in 1813 when other mill owners petitioned for improvements in the navigation of the river. The legislation starts:

> *Whereas David Lydig, Herman Vosburgh, James Bathgate, Peter and George Lorillard and Peter A Memer, owners of manufactories established at and near the head of the tide waters of a certain creek or river called the Bronx, situate*[d] *in the county of Weslchester, have by their petition to the legislature, represented that the navigation of said creek is susceptible of great improvement, by certain alterations in the course thereof, and that they are willing to defray the expenses incident to such improvements: Therefore, Be it enacted...that...appointed commissioners...survey and examine the said creek from its outlet to the oil mill owned by the Bronx river paint company.*[59]

Not stated in this documentation is what the obstacles to navigation were. Was it the discoloration of the river by the discharged pigments? Was the "obstruction" actually corrected by straightening the channel and thereby increasing the speed of the river's flow?[60] This remains a mystery.

BOLTON BLEACHERY: 1840S TO 1930S

Henry B. Bolton died on December 19, 1895, at the age of sixty-five, leaving "a considerable fortune." By the time of his death, his company, the Bronx Company, was more than a half century old. Its primary mill was originally built on the Bronx River as the first building in what became a prosperous village: Bronxdale. In 1885, the mill and factory were displaced from Bronxdale and moved to West Farms at about 175th Street as a result of the taking of land on which it was situated, by eminent domain, to form Bronx Park.[61] The City of New York completed its condemnation procedure in 1889 when it paid the Boltons $267,324.40 in damages, as authorized under the Laws of 1884.[62]

The Bolton Dam, the Bronx Company or the Bronx Bleachery (all used to describe the same enterprise that bleached and dyed cotton) was built in the 1840s and was located on the river until after World War I,[63] but it had an uneven record of prosperity. The company went into

Two dams with an island in the middle located in the Bronx Zoo are all that is left of the Bolton Bleachery and of Bronxdale. The island in the middle affords portage for downriver canoe trips. This is the dam on the west side of the Bronx River looking north. *Photo by Maarten de Kadt.*

bankruptcy in 1878. A dispute over A.C. Chandler's rights to cut ice from the millpond caused some of the firm's difficulties.[64] Perhaps so did competition from cotton processors in Massachusetts cotton factories. Nonetheless, the Bronx Bleachery managed to continue functioning into the twentieth century, using the river's flowing water as its power source.

Both the mill and Bronxdale community, in which it was situated, contributed to the pollution of the Bronx River. The workers and their families around this mill probably deposited some of their own bodily wastes into the river, which was already becoming burdened by sewage wastes. It is also likely that rain washed their wastes into the river. The Bronx Bleachery clearly contributed to the river's degradation, as it used chemicals that older mills did not. Water was used to wash out both acids and alkalines used in the bleaching process. In addition, the mill works dyed the cotton, introducing a new spectrum of chemicals that would have added color to the river. Undoubtedly the washing process sped these chemicals into the river causing harm downstream.

This is the dam of the Bolton Bleachery on the east side of the Bronx River looking north. *Photo by Maarten de Kadt.*

From the perspective of its environmental effect on the river, the Bolton Dam story is complicated. The Bolton Dam was relatively far downstream and could not have been responsible for the ample upstream wastes. While the Bronx Bleachery undoubtedly caused some harm to the Bronx River Watershed, human wastes produced by an influx of people were a larger contributor to the river's serious late nineteenth-century pollution.

Today the only physical remnants of the Bronx Company are the milldam in what is now the Bronx Zoo (North Bolton Dam) and some dam foundations in West Farms (South Bolton Dam).

OTHER MILLDAMS

The approximately twelve mill sites on the Bronx River changed hands and names, making it difficult to determine if twelve is the correct number.[65] There are the four mill sites in what is now the Bronx: Lorillard,

Behind the Scarsdale Train Station, this dam presents a perfect opportunity for a local park. This was the site of Crawford's Saw Mill. *Photo by Maarten de Kadt.*

Delancey/Lydig and two Bolton sites. In addition there was the paint company somewhere in what is now the Bronx Zoo. Within what is now Westchester, there were at least seven sites: two mills, a grist- and sawmill, owned by Ruben and Thomas Wright,[66] both now under the Kensico Reservoir; Horton's Tannery Mill in White Plains; Haubold's Gunpowder Mill in Hartsdale; Crawford's Saw Mill in Scarsdale; the Old Stone Mill in Tuckahoe; and Swain's Cutlery Mill in Bronxville.

Because they processed organic materials, the grist- and sawmills were unlikely to have caused long-term problems for the river (though tannin in lumber could have been an environmental problem for the Bronx River). Snuff is also an organic product. To the extent it has any residue, if piled up on land or if dumped in the river, it decomposes. And while ammonia has been used on tobacco products, it was not available on a commercial scale until World War I, when it was introduced as a constituent part of explosive devices.

The impacts of bleach, gunpowder, tannery, stone, paint and rubber mills are different. In each of these industries, it is likely that chemicals were used either in the manufacturing process or in the lubrication of the equipment. These chemicals were likely to have caused harm to the river. At issue then for each mill is: what were the quantities of these chemicals in relation to the river's ability to absorb or disperse them?

While the waste of industry contributed to the pollution of the Bronx River, it is likely, as with the earlier mills, that the humans (both slave and free) who worked in and around the river's mills contributed human waste as well. As more dams were built, they further restricted the movement of migratory fish and caused increased silt deposits in the riverbed. By the end of the nineteenth century, these environmental incursions all added up.

The collection of mills along the Bronx River was part of the nation's industrialization process. Early grist- and sawmills initially produced products for the use of the local farmers. As the opportunity presented itself, these mills produced goods for faraway markets. The cotton, tobacco, paint, rubber and gunpowder mills' primary purpose was to serve remote markets. They represent a transformation to industrial capitalism from the earlier mercantile period. They increased the amount of waste producers disposed of in the river.

COAL GASIFICATION

Sometime prior to 1881, a manufactured gas plant was constructed at East 173rd Street.[67] Manufactured gas, a derivative of coal, was used for heating, lighting and cooking in the late 1800s and the early 1900s until other lighting and heating technologies became dominant. The manufactured gas was distributed to Bronx residents through a system of pipes and meters. By 1895, this plant serviced thirty-five miles of gas mains.[68] The plant produced manufactured gas until 1912. Northern Union Gas Company acquired the facilities in 1897. Con Edison took over in 1936 when it acquired Northern Union Gas's assets.

The gas manufacturing process required water to produce steam, with the Bronx River as its likely source. The Bronx River was also a convenient depository for production wastes, including cyanide and other metals the plant may have used or produced as byproducts resulting from gas making. The effluent from the gas manufacturing process caused serious river contamination, leading to complaints by local residents to the Health Department:

> *The chief causes of the pollution and of the odors therefrom are the waste products of the Bronx Wool and Leather Company and of the Northern Gas-light Company. In the latter works the old-fashioned dry-lime process is employed, and there are no means for storing the ammonia water produced in them. This water, with all the impurities it contains and carries with it, is allowed to run into the river, depositing the heavy materials on the banks, which for a distance above and below the gas-works are covered with refuse…The Inspector recommends that the Northern Gas-Light Company be required to abandon the dry-lime process and adopt the iron process in its stead; that they be required to provide suitable wells for the ammonia water and to prevent the overflow of the tar wells running into the river, and that the surface waters of the works be carried into a drain well, closed by gates, which shall be only raised at high tide, thus enabling matters hitherto deposited to be carried off.*[69]

Here is another example of an industrial facility simultaneously benefiting from the Bronx River in the service of its community while damaging the river at the same time.

The existence of this plant caused local community concern in 2002, ninety years after the plant ceased operation. Contaminants from the gas manufacturing process were discovered under Starlight Park, the site the former plant had occupied. Their discovery was triggered just after the nearby Sheridan Expressway was repaved, new storm water drainage was installed and the park was being prepared for renovation.

Industries advanced to using other sources of energy. They no longer used flowing water. The tobacco, rubber, cotton and gas industries moved to other locations where fossil fuel power (coal and petroleum) was a more convenient source of energy. With their departure, industry declined further in the Bronx River Valley. In the 1800s, the Bronx River's developing industry surely contributed to its pollution, reflecting industrialization in the rest of the country. There are, however, other more prevalent causes of the river's pollution during this time, including new railroads and rapidly expanding population growth.

Chapter 4
A Place to Live

During the fourth and final economic period studied in this book, a period in which industry largely moved to other locations, residents in the Bronx River Valley began consuming products made elsewhere, a pattern that continues into the present.

Population would not have grown as dramatically as it did in outlying Westchester (including the territory that became the Bronx) without railroads. They brought industry, thus furthering the development of the third economic period, even though much of the industry eventually relocated. They also brought people. Railroads negatively affected the Bronx River environment in three ways: as more people moved north of New York City, the environmental load on land and water also expanded; railroad activities emitted their own form of pollution that ended up in the Bronx River; and the building of the railroads resulted in channeling the river.

Railroads: Transportation Innovation Brings Pollution, 1841

Railroads, powered by a mobile form of the steam engine, first used in England in 1804, were indeed a major transportation innovation, enabling areas far from central cities to develop. The New York and

Harlem Railroad first crossed the Harlem River in 1841. Originally operating as horse-drawn carriages on rails, it connected New York City in lower Manhattan with its suburbs farther north. As a steam engine–drawn passenger railroad, coal ash, slurry and cinders replaced the earlier railroad's animal waste. Its locomotion depended on an ample water source. Then as now, its railroad ties were covered with creosote, which is a potent carcinogen. When Irish laborers eventually enabled the railroad to reach the Bronx River near Fordham, in late 1841, the river undoubtedly became a water source for steam engines. From Fordham, the New York and Harlem Railroad went up the Bronx River Valley, reaching White Plains in 1844. Construction of the railroad included straightening the river's course to a channel-like canal. This straightening of the river increased the river's velocity, decreased its mixing qualities and therefore reduced its ability to absorb pollutants. It is very likely that the river was the recipient of at least some of the railroad's coal ash, slurry and cinders from both the byproducts of combustion and from the bed of the new train tracks.[70]

These railroads brought markets closer to Westchester County, promoting industrial operation. As landownership was divided, new homes were built and farming declined, Westchester's increasing number of residents began to depend on food and other products produced elsewhere. Not only were the markets for products produced in Westchester easier to get to because of the railroads, markets producing goods elsewhere could ship them to Westchester more conveniently. As a result, in the late 1800s, population steadily grew along newly developed transportation routes. At the same time, however, the success of industry elsewhere, along with the development of power sources not dependent on a river's flowing water, led to a decline of industry in the territory north of New York City.

Railroads, including New York City's early 1900s rapid transit system, became important promoters of population growth in the counties north of Manhattan. A second railroad that infringed on the Bronx River, the Harlem River & Port Chester Railroad, began operating in 1873. Construction of this railroad, overseen by the New York, New Haven & Hartford Railroad, included building a string of highly attractive passenger stations in 1908, famous for their renowned architect, Cass Gilbert.

Overlooking Concrete Plant Park, the vacant Westchester Avenue train station, Cass Gilbert Train Station, owned by Amtrak, stands in ruin. Looking at its decaying Spanish tile roof, one can only imagine its original elegance. *Photo by Maarten de Kadt.*

Together these railroads facilitated the movement of people from New York City into what was then Westchester County. People with enough money could live north of Manhattan and use these newly built railroads for an easy commute to work as part of a much broader dispersal of population into the nearby New York City suburbs.[71] Large numbers of new residents in the rapidly developing territory north of New York City, and the sewage waste associated with their presence, greatly contributed to the pollution of the Bronx River and many other New York City waterways.

POPULATION INCREASE

In the last half of the 1800s, population grew rapidly in the territory just north of Manhattan (see Tables 1 and 2). Parts of Westchester County were first annexed to New York City in 1874, forming the 23rd and 24th Wards on the territory west of the Bronx River. The territory east of the Bronx River was annexed to the city in 1895, extending the 24th Ward. In the period between 1840 and 1890, the population in the territory west of the river nearly doubled.

Table 1: Westchester Population 1731–1840

Year	Population	Percent Change
1731	6,033	
1771	21,745	260
1786	20,554	-5
1790	24,003	17
1800	27,423	14
1810	30,272	10
1835	37,791	25
1840	48,686	29

(Bolton Jr. 1848, vol. 1, xiii)

Table 2: The Bronx's Population 1875-2000

Year	Population	Percent Change	Percent West of the Bronx River
1875	36,194		Wards 23 and 24
1890	88,908	146	Wards 23 and 24
1900	200,507	126	89
1910	430,980	115	89
1920	732,016	70	91
1930	1,265,258	73	79
1950	1,451,277	15	73
1970	1,471,701	1	67
1980	1,168,972	-21	58
2000	1,332,650	14	60

Note: In 1874, territory west of the Bronx River that became Wards 23 and 24 was annexed to New York City. In 1895, territory east of the Bronx River became part of New York City. Greater New York City was established in 1898, at which time the territories ceded earlier received the name the "Borough of the Bronx River" or "the Bronx." (Gonzalez, *The Bronx*, 17, 4)

An oft-told story[72] about the population increase on the mainland peninsula is about Robert Campbell and Edward Willis. In 1860, they purchased eighty acres in South Morrisania (an area that later would be part of the 23rd Ward) and subdivided it into one thousand twenty- by one-hundred-foot lots. To prepare for the one thousand houses, they leveled the hills and filled the hollows. This process usually meant a gentle sloping of the land toward a water body to promote the runoff of rainfall. In this case, the runoff probably went south toward the East River, increasing its environmental burden, which was not irrelevant to the Bronx River, as both water bodies' waters mix together through tidal action. It is likely that these houses were provided with privies to accommodate human waste. New privies were established when filled privies were closed and covered up, or privies were emptied to be used again. Could their contents have been used as fertilizer or were they transported to a water body? Rain washed away waste whenever a privy failed. The sloping and grading occurred wherever tracts of new homes were developed, as they were in the Bronx River Valley.[73]

Population was also increasing north of what is now New York City, as indicated by towns that were achieving sufficient size to incorporate (see Table 3). Size was one reason to incorporate. So was avoiding inclusion in Andrew Haswell Green's[74] scheme to create a greater New York City. In the late 1800s, "Mount Vernon and the surrounding areas of Eastchester…[established] their own economic base of both industry and commerce. In 1892 Eastchester voters chose not to join the New York City borough of the Bronx, but to incorporate Mount Vernon as a city."[75] Bronxville's 1898 incorporation accomplished a similar end.

As with the development farther downstream, these growing communities along the Bronx River contributed sewage to the river. They also increased the need for ample amounts of drinking water.

Table 3: Bronx River Village Incorporations in Westchester County, New York

Village	Incorporation Date
Yonkers	1855
New Rochelle	1858
White Plains	1866
Mount Vernon	1892
Bronxville	1898
Tuckahoe	1903
Scarsdale	1915

(Jackson 1985, 321; "Village of Scarsdale, http://www.scarsdale.com/Home/HistoryofScarsdale/tabid/183/Default.aspx; "Historical Treasures of Westchester County," http://www.westchesterarchives.com/HT/muni/yonkers/yonkers.htm and http://www.westchesterarchives.com/HT/muni/eastch/eastchester.html; Mount Vernon: Ultan 2009, 189).

Kensico Dam

As we've seen, New York City had been looking to the north for drinking water since 1799. With the completion of the Croton Reservoir in 1842, the city finally had a reliable source of drinking water. With the city's continued increase in population and in geographic area, more water was needed.

> *By 1881, in the midst of another water shortage, the city was putting* [its] *latest plan* [to provide the city with additional drinking water] *in motion with the construction of the first Kensico Reservoir to serve the newly annexed Westchester towns of Morrisania, Kingsbridge and West Farms.*[76]

When the first Kensico dam, a forty-five-foot-high masonry dam on the Bronx River, was completed in 1885, it constricted the river's flow while becoming a drinking water source for the 23rd and 24th Ward communities in the Northern Annex. In 1915, the completion of a larger Kensico Dam further diminished the river's flow. "New York City's demand for water continued to rise and the construction of the Kensico Dam diverted the upper reaches of the Bronx River into the reservoir, cutting the river's water flow by approximately 25 percent in 1915."[77]

The Kensico Dam hydraulically separates the original Bronx River headwaters from today's Bronx River, but the headwaters behind the dam are not the only source of the river's water. The river's long, narrow watershed drains into the river as well. The reservoir created by the Kensico Dam drowned the village of Kensico, terminated the operation of two water-powered mills and reduced the river's flow. The reduction in the river's flow further reduced the river's ability to cleanse itself, as wastes could not as quickly be flushed into the larger body water, the East River.

As part of the developing New York City water supply, the dam created a reservoir of more than thirty billion gallons of drinkable water. The drinking water delivered to Bronx communities and used by its

Kensico Dam, Valhalla, New York. This masonry dam was constructed between 1909 and 1915. It replaced an earlier dam constructed in 1885. The dam is 1,825 feet long and stands 307 feet above its base. *Photo by Maarten de Kadt.*

The Kensico Dam created a 30.6 billion gallon reservoir (equivalent to about a thirty day supply of New York City's drinking water) used to move about 90 percent of the city's drinking water from Delaware and the Catskills to New York City. The reservoir's watershed—the original Bronx River source—provides the city with just under 2 percent of its drinking water. The Dam House, in the background on the right of this photo, sits at the western end of the dam. *Photo by Maarten de Kadt.*

residents needed someplace to go. After it was used, it became sewage, adding to the environmental burden in local water bodies. Today the reservoir, correctly described as a "balancing reservoir," transmits 90 percent of New York City's drinking water to the city from the Catskill and Delaware Watersheds. This 2,081-acre reservoir, at the bottom of its own watershed, collects just under 2 percent of the city's drinking water from original Bronx River sources, while it transmits much larger quantities of water to the city from somewhere else.[78]

There are two ironies here: just as the Bronx River became as polluted as it has ever been, the city began siphoning off its headwaters as a drinking water source, and just as the Bronx River is in greatest need of cleanup, its flow is diminished by this dam, thus further reducing the river's own ability of self-cleansing.

RIVERS RECEIVE WASTE: THE SECOND BENCHMARK, 1896

By the end of the 1800s, the river was no longer "as clear as spring water."[79] In 1896, the Bronx Valley Sewer Commission declared it to be an "open sewer." The commission's description is graphic:

> *Into this stream of varying flow all kinds of sewage refuse and factory waste finds its way. Barn yards, privies, cesspools, and gas house refuge, the watery part of White Plains' sewage disposal works, drains from houses in Tuckahoe, Bronxville, Mount Vernon, Woodlawn and Williamsbridge deposit their unsanitary and foul-smelling contributions. The observation of the Commission and the complaints of citizens at the several hearings all confirm the undisputed fact that the Bronx has become* "an open sewer."... [A]*ll agreed that a sewer with the proper outlet was a necessity.*[80]

Pollution of the region's waterways, however, was not unique to the Bronx River. Dams on the Saw Mill River had to be removed for sanitary reasons in 1892, enabling that river to better perform its natural cleansing function.[81] The East River was a receptor of the city's wastes. "Blood and entrails...were usually dumped into the East River at the city inspector's pier. Despite the action of tide and currents, a viscous accumulation had so filled the channel that it inhibited navigation."[82] The nearby New Jersey Passaic River's pollution "by waste from breweries, tanneries, and other factories, as well as by organic filth from various sewers, had destroyed real estate values along the river valley."[83]

Policy makers knew the river was polluted, and they knew the complex causes: industry, railroads, dams, river straightening and a half century of population increase. Motivation to actively clean the Bronx River and the other water bodies would require a sea change in the general understanding of the role of rivers in their watersheds.

Chapter 5
Reclaiming the River

By the beginning of the twentieth century, the Bronx River had become a much less important source of power. Its mills were either closed, soon to be closed or operating using a different power source. Small industry still existed in the Bronx River Watershed, however, and continued to contribute effluents. As an open sewer, the Bronx River attracted the attention of policy makers who worked to improve the water's quality. Sewers were being built using the best engineering available in that day, and they moved some sewage into larger bodies of water. However, these pipes would leave the legacy of a combined sewer and storm water infrastructure, incapable of moving all the sewage to treatment plants especially when it rains, causing water pollution today.

During the century following the Bronx Valley Sewer Commission's branding the river an open sewer, the river was replete with projects to improve it and with people enjoying it. But with further decline of industry and widespread disregard of what was going on, improvement was unsteady. Over time, neglect invited dumping of cars, washing machines and other debris. But even during the worst of times, parts of the Bronx River remained a desirable venue, attracting the attention of ordinary people.

Pleasant Pursuits

In 1888, after considerable negotiation with property owners and the invocation of eminent domain, Bronx Park was formed. Most of the park was inside what was then New York City's 24th Ward. Some of it was on the eastern or Westchester side of the river. The site was to become the New York Botanical Garden in the north and the Bronx Zoological Garden in the south. Both of these bucolic gardens would be visited by many millions of people annually. However, these places of obvious beauty were not without environmental costs. Zoo wastes, especially those from outdoor animals, were washed by rain into the river until the first decade of the twenty-first century.[84] The river, however, enriched the beauty of these wonderful parks.

At about the same time, concurrent with substantial French immigration, a number of restaurants opened on barges and houseboats along the Bronx River. A wooded section of Bronx Park, north of the botanical garden, that hikers along the river come to visit today is called "French Charlie's," after a restaurant that is now long since gone. One rhapsodic 1892 essay that describes the joy of dining next to the flowing water of the Bronx River highlighted the beauty of the river and the wonders of a peaceful place to dine despite its compromised state:

> *There is a quality which one never sees in nature until she has been rough handled by man and has outlived the usage. It is the picturesque… Then came the long interval that succeeds that deadly conversion of the once sweet farming lands, redolent with clover, into that barren waste—suburban property. The conflict that had lasted since the days when the pioneer's axe first running through the stillness of the forest was nearly over; nature saw her chance, took revenge, and began that regeneration which is exclusively her own. The weeds ran riot; tall grasses shot up in the sunlight, concealing the once well trimmed banks; and great tangles of underbrush and alders made lusty efforts to hide traces of man's unceasing cruelty. Lastly came this little group of poor people from the Seine and the Marne and lent a helping hand, bringing with them something of their old life at home,—their boats, and landings, patched up water-stairs, fences, arbors, and vine covered cottages,—unconsciously*

A footbridge near Woodlawn shows how bucolic the river was in 1881 even during a period of railroad building, industrialization and population growth. *Stephen Jenkins's* The Story of the Bronx: From the Purchase Made by the Dutch from the Indians in 1639 to the Present Day.

> *completing the picture and adding the one thing needful—a human touch. So, nature having outlived the wrongs of a hundred years, has here with busy fingers so woven a web of weed, moss, trailing vine, and low branching tree that there is seen a newer and more transit quality in her beauty which, for want of a better term, we call the picturesque.*[85]

The author was aware of the damage that had been done to the Bronx River but found an oasis of beauty in spite of the obvious pollution.

Sewers

The Bronx River's pollution needed to be abated, but it would not be until 1911 that a major sewer was built coming from the north to Yonkers, turning west and emptying into the Hudson River Estuary. Waste from the northern part of the river's watershed was sent into another, larger watershed.[86] Prior to the building of sewers, rain moved waste into the water body at the bottom of the watershed. When it rains, storm water moves pollution downhill into water bodies. One need only look at watershed maps to determine which waterway was the recipient of this offal. Along with the building of sewers, storm drains were built along roads in the watersheds, sending thousands of gallons of contaminated water from "non-point sources"—roads, sidewalks, parking lots, gardens and the like—into the nearby waterways. Today, much of that additional water (but not all of it) is moved to a sewage treatment plant in a combined storm drain and sewer system.

Sewers enabled the moving of waste out of a watershed. The integrity of a single watershed was breached. The term "sewershed" came to mean the area from which sewage is collected. That area may coincide with an actual watershed. While it is the case that there can be no clean body of water at the bottom of a dirty watershed, when sewers collect rain water and sewage together and move them from one watershed to another, the second watershed, no matter what its environmental condition, is contaminated by the first. Thus there can be no clean body of water at the bottom of multiple, interconnected, dirty watersheds.

Over time, New York City systematized the building of sewers. When the Dutch arrived in 1624, Broad Street in lower Manhattan was a flowing brook. In order to promote commerce, the Dutch excavated this brook into a canal. The canal became a logical place to dispose of human waste. When the British arrived in 1664, the flowing brook had become an open sewer. As a result, the British covered the sewer with a stone roof, making Broad Street New York City's first sewer.

In the following years, a patchwork of sewers was built in the city to move human waste to the nearby bodies of water. In the 1800s, sewers were built on an ad hoc, catch-as-catch-can, the-property-owner-pays-the-costs basis, in sharp contrast to the building of the Croton Reservoir, the Kensico Reservoir and the larger water delivery system that was built as an overarching system. It was not until the professionalization of sewer building by qualified engineers after the mid-nineteenth century that sewer building became systematized under the aegis of government agencies. One of the first trunk sewers, used to collect the waste from multiple individual sewers, was the 1809 Canal Street Sewer in Manhattan, flowing into the Hudson River. This sewer was dug after the filling of the Collect Pond, one of Manhattan's original drinking water sources that had become polluted by a beer distillery and a local tannery. The Canal Street Sewer was an open trench sixteen feet wide in the middle of the street. Between 1845 and 1855, 105 miles of sewers were built between Manhattan's Sixtieth Street and the Battery from the Hudson to the East River. In 1857, the New York State legislature created the Brooklyn Board of Sewer Commissioners. In 1866, the legislature passed "An Act to Create a Metropolitan Sanitary District and Board of Health Therein." Westchester was included in the act's purview. By 1865, construction began on sewers between Twenty-eighth Street and Ninety-first Street between Fifth Avenue and the East River in seven separate sewer districts.[87]

This systematization did not reach the Northern Annex until the early 1890s, when two sewer districts were formed in the 23rd Ward.[88] Before 1874, just more than three miles of brick and pipe sewers were built in what was to become the 23rd and 24th Wards of New York City's first Northern Annex. Records of sewer construction began to accumulate after 1874 for the same territory west of the Bronx River. In the seventeen-year period between 1874 and 1890, thirty-three miles of sewers (two miles per year) were placed in the 23rd and 24th Wards. That pace increased between 1891 and 1895 with the construction of thirty-eight miles of sewers (just under eight miles per year). Between 1896 and 1897, thirty more miles of sewers were built. A great trunk sewer was built under the Bronx section of Broadway between 1901 and 1904 (capturing Tibbets Brook's flow and directing it to the Spuyten Duyvill outlet sewer). In 1912, the Bronx's Jerome Avenue was "almost impassable, owing to regrading, sewering, etc."[89]

Treatment of sewer waste did not come to the Bronx until 1937, when the Ward's Island Sewage Plant began processing waste from the western section of the borough. The Bronx River Watershed's sewage was not treated until 1952 with the opening of the Hunts Point Water Treatment Plant. There are now fourteen water treatment plants in New York City and eleven serving Westchester County,[90] with the result that most sewage is captured and treated. However, in addition to the legal combined storm water and sewer outlets, there are still illegal connections that discharge sewage directly into local waterways, including the Bronx River. Combining storm drains and sewage pipes was state of the art in the late 1800s. Combined storm-water and sewage pipes today are a primary cause of urban water pollution, especially when it rains. Sewage plants and some of the pipes leading to them have not been designed to manage the increased flow of combined storm water and sewage. The untreated excess is still directed to nearby water bodies. Adequate management of storm water is both a political and a technical problem and will have to be addressed in the future.

THE BRONX RIVER PARKWAY

Sewers were an important infrastructural element in removing upstream waste from the Bronx River, especially at a time when the river had been overwhelmed by sewage. The building of the Bronx River Parkway with its greenway buffer was intended to block debris from reaching the river. It also exacerbated the problem by straightening the river, as river bends, oxbows and rapids facilitate the mixing of water and increase oxygenation, promoting the river's ability to degrade waste.

In 1918, the Bronx Parkway Commission, reacting to the open sewer that the Bronx River had become, described its primary mission as river cleanup:

> *20 years and more ago, the rapid spread of the City of New York to the north, in what is now the Borough of The Bronx, and the increasing population of the Westchester communities of Mount Vernon, Bronxville, Tuckahoe, Crestwood, Scarsdale, Hartsdale, White Plains, North White Plains, and Valhalla, lying in the Bronx River valley, as well as the inevitable consequences of unchecked pollution to the Bronx River by those populous and politically independent centers along its banks, gradually transformed what was once a small river of pure water into a foul stream. Too polluted to sustain aquatic life, it became a menace to the health of the community, obstructed as it was at many places by ever-growing masses of debris and rubbish. Periodically floods back the foul waters upon the adjacent lowlands; or, sometimes by their force swept the unwholesome obstructions down stream and, subsiding, deposited them some distance from the normal River channel or floated the whole foul mass into the beautiful lakes* [mill dam impoundments?] *which constitute one of the greatest charms of Bronx Park.*[91]

The Bronx Parkway Commission, established in 1907, purchased land it needed to construct the parkway. For the properties it could not purchase, it used the powers of the state, through eminent domain, to obtain the required land for the parkway's right-of-way. One property obtained through eminent domain was owned by Bart Badaracco, whose grandson tells the story: "God bless my tough Grandpa, Bart Badaracco, for defying those responsible for ripping him off by taking his houses and rolling them up into Yonkers. I'm sure that if he could have similarly rolled his topsoil he'd have taken that too."[92] Not all those who had their homesteads threatened by the oncoming construction of the Bronx River Parkway moved their houses to nearby Yonkers. Some merely rolled them up the hill where they can be seen to this day. Of the 1,315 parcels of land the commission had to acquire, 463 were obtained through condemnation procedures within the state's power of eminent domain.[93] One of those, just north of 236th Street, was Grandpa Badaracco's land.

The parkway forced the removal of most industry along its banks. Also removed were the shantytowns that had grown up along the river. This displacement was intended to create the parkland buffer on both sides of the river and thus keep debris from finding its way into the river. Constructing the parkway as a buffer protected the river from environmental damage. However, the project could not cleanse the entire watershed, thus the river remained quite dirty because some sewers continued to drain into the river.

As seen in before and after photographs, the Bronx Parkway Commission Report leaves no doubt that the river, by 1917, remained in dire need of cleanup. One photograph notably depicts numerous obstructions under a bridge. A year later, the second photograph shows that the obstructions were gone and the river was again running freely. The report also contains a photo of a 1918 sewer depositing its effluent into the river at 235th Street near Bullard Avenue. This source of pollution was removed as the parkway was constructed,[94] but there were other sewer overflows into the Bronx River that were not removed or connected to the Bronx Valley sewer pipe. This overflow would be reestablished at a later date. The parkway only touched the Northern Bronx, coming nowhere near to the mouth of the Bronx River where there were four sewer overflow pipes depicted on a 1905 New York Harbor & Vicinity map.[95] Today,

The Bronx Parkway Commission reported that it corrected the pollution from this outlet by 1918, and it may have been. *Report of the Bronx Parkway Commission.*

During the 1950s, with the reconstruction of the Bronx River Parkway, new riverside parks were also built. This storm drain outlet is in the same place as the one depicted in the *Report of the Bronx Parkway Commission.* The apartment buildings in the background were built subsequent to the earlier image. Unfortunately, this section of the Bronx River remains an environmental hot spot. We exchange our problems instead of eliminating them. *Photo by Maarten de Kadt.*

An obstructed river channel under a bridge in 1917. While the source document for this and the next photo does not indicate location, it is likely to be the bridge just north of the Woodlawn Station. *Report of the Bronx Parkway Commission.*

Cleared river channel under the same bridge in 1918. *Report of the Bronx Parkway Commission.*

Bronx River Channel running clear, just north of the Woodlawn Station in 2011. This image is taken from the west side of the bridge. The previous two images seem to have been taken from the east side of the same bridge. *Photo by Maarten de Kadt.*

three combined sewer overflows still exist south of Bruckner Boulevard at the mouth of the Bronx River (HP-008, HP-009 and HP-010. HP means Hunts Point, referring to the water treatment plant to which the sewage would otherwise go when it is not raining).

The construction of the Bronx River Parkway did have at least two unintended environmental effects on the watershed. First, the river was again rechanneled, both to accommodate the new parkway and the repositioning of the 1911 sewer pipe to a "more economical location."[96] Shifting the river's course (once again) both straightened and, in a few places, added turns to some of the canal-like features created when the railroad was constructed.

Second, as part of its beautification effort, some land adjacent to the river was filled in. Ironically, by filling in a number of wetlands,[97] those natural low-lying areas could no longer help control flooding. Filling in of wetlands occurred when their value as animal habitat and as

Flooding is still a periodic problem in the Bronx River Watershed. In March 2007, severe flooding occurred in the Bronx River Forest section of the New York Botanical Garden. *Photo by Bronx River Alliance.*

areas capable of absorbing potential flood water was, at that time, not appreciated. The Bronx River's periodic flooding today is likely a partial result of the loss of wetlands in the Bronx River Watershed.

Paradoxically, the building of the Bronx River Parkway to block waste from overwhelming the Bronx River increased the possibility that cars would become a major new source of both water and air pollution. The commission recognized that "the City of New York has another vital need for such reclamation of the valley of the Bronx River as would provide a permanent outlet for its fast-growing motor traffic, from the cramped and growing metropolis to the open country to the north."[98]

With the coming of the auto age, moving cars was becoming the primary purpose for road building.[99] Parkways were one of the forms that road building took and the Bronx River Parkway was one of the first with limited access and egress, built to be attractive and to permanently increase existing parkland. However, cars became a source of pollution for rivers and streams in at least three ways. First, their fluids (gas and oil) wash into water bodies as runoff. Second, car bodies were dumped in rivers, as was the case with the Bronx River. Finally, passengers often jettison their garbage out of the windows of their moving vehicles, despoiling the landscape and the river. Building the parkway and its associated greenway buffer zone did clean the river, but increased automobile usage caused its own form of environmental harm.

Social Differentiation along the Bronx River

Between 1920 and 1950, the population in the counties through which the Bronx River runs increased about twofold (see Table 2 in Chapter 4 and Table 4). New residents of the Bronx during this period included Italians, Germans, Jews, African Americans, Latinos and others. Folks were looking for affordable, decent homes in a stable community and a transportation network that would conveniently take them to work. In this period, the housing stock increased, schools were built, civic facilities were constructed, the first Yankee Stadium was completed, the Bronx Courthouse was built and transportation was improved. It was an era of boom in the 1920s, of bust in the 1930s and of war in the 1940s. It was a period during which progressive movements including the Communist Party and socialist movements of the United States flourished in the Bronx. In the words of Lloyd Ultan, the Bronx historian:

> *The image of the Bronx in the minds of people who did not live there was largely positive. It was a borough of neighborhoods, overwhelmingly Jewish, but with significant numbers of Irish, Italians, and other groups, but all shared middle-class values. It was a borough filled with high-class apartment houses with the latest amenities, and neat single-family homes. In an era of hard times and economic uncertainty, it exuded an aura of stability, a place where people went to work every day and enjoyed simple pleasures.*[100]

Table 4: Westchester Population 1900-2000

Year	Population	Percent Change
1900	184,257	
1910	283,055	54
1920	344,436	22
1930	520,947	51
1940	573,558	10
1950	625,816	9
1960	808,981	29
1970	894,104	11
1980	866,599	-3
1990	874,866	1
2000	923,459	6

(Westchester.gov, "Databook Westchester County")

However, this nascent multicultural/multiethnic borough was being undercut by the Home Owners' Loan Corporation (HOLC), established in 1933 to evaluate real estate nationally for potential mortgagors, including, initially HOLC itself. HOLC rated geographic regions on an "A" to "D" scale. Their evaluations were not based solely on the condition of the real estate in question. HOLC used racial and ethnic profiling of residents in their grading of communities.

> *The First grade (also A and green) areas were described as new, homogeneous, and "in demand as residential locations in good times and bad." Homogeneous meant "American business and professional men." Jewish neighborhoods, or even those with an "infiltration of Jews," could not be considered "best" any more than they could be considered "American."*
>
> *The Second security grade (blue) went to "still desirable" areas that had "reached their peak," but were expected to remain stable for many years. The Third grade (yellow or "C") neighborhoods were usually described as "definitely declining," while the Fourth grade (red) neighborhoods were defined as areas "in which the things taking place in C areas have already happened."*[101]

Because of the way it colored its maps, HOLC set in motion the now illegal practice of what came to be called "red lining." Banks and insurance companies quickly began to use the practice to delineate areas in which they would offer no mortgage or insurance coverage. The 1938 Bronx HOLC map is mostly yellow and red, with a bit of blue and green tossed in. The upscale area of Riverdale is green. Communities along the Bronx River were given the lowest ratings, as yellow and red. Sound View and Morrisania (areas along the Bronx River in the South Bronx) were rated D, the fourth and lowest grade, by HOLC. What is now Shoelace Park (north of Bronx Park) was C rated. Only slightly farther north, however, southern Westchester areas along the river (Bronxville and parts of Yonkers) were A rated.[102]

The completion of the Westchester portion of the Bronx River Parkway established a suburban transportation model based on an individual modality: the automobile rather than the train. Mass transportation (the train) was constructed for Bronx residents while private transportation was preferred by upper income Westchester residents. Once it was the train that was the fastest mode of transportation in and out of the city. Now it was the car. Four roadways facilitating auto travel to Westchester County were completed by the 1930s: the Saw Mill River Parkway, the Hutchinson River Parkway, the Taconic Parkway and the Cross County Parkway.[103]

For the more wealthy, automobiles, and for the less wealthy, subway trains, along with their associated elevated trains, were part of the increasingly regressive social differentiation along the Bronx River that would intensify as time went on. Westchester, with the Bronx River Parkway (and the other new roadways) and its greater distance from the center of the New York City business district, became upscale. The Bronx, nearer to the city and without the greenway buffer along the parkway (that buffer stops in the northern part of the Bronx), became more commercial with a larger population supported by fewer government resources.

Despite development of these spatial inequalities during this period, good things were happening along the river. The Bronx International Exposition opened in 1917 near West Farms Square in the Bronx. A few years later, it became the Starlight Park Amusement Park, sporting a large swimming pool, an arena called the New York Coliseum, a roller coaster and other entertainment facilities used by the local population.[104] At the beginning of World War II, "Starlight Park and the Coliseum were taken over by the War Department as a facility to store and repair trucks."[105] Farther upstream, there were recreational events. On Saturday, April 6, 1935, the fishermen of the Bronx gathered around 233rd Street to fish for trout. As reported by the *New York Times*, "Five hundred and sixty sleek, brown trout, living up to the implications of their pugnacious lower jaws, battled scores of urban anglers to a standstill yesterday in the pleasant shallows of the Bronx River."[106] Citizens and public officials are pictured attempting to snag trout released into the Bronx River by the State Conservation Commission.

While many were unaware of the river's existence, at least one former Bronx resident revels in its memory. As a young ten-year-old boy in 1940, Nat Yalowitz remembers running freely in the area of Bronx Park and its river. The park and the river were "another world." They were an escape from the city's "concrete jungle" and from the Depression. Yalowitz remembers swimming in the river, but "I did not drink the water." He recalls paying a very expensive fifty cents to rent a boat and row on the millpond north of the 181st Street dam. And most importantly, Yalowitz remembers the river being "clean"—whatever that meant to a ten-year-old boy.[107]

Another former Bronx resident living farther north than Yalowitz, Jack Raskin, remembers that at about the same time he drank the Bronx

River's water. As a twelve-year-old boy, Raskin also fondly recalls playing in and around the Bronx River near the Westchester border.[108]

But with the increasing population all along the Bronx River, its waters again became polluted. Yet another former Bronx resident, Joyce Miller, remembers standing on the 174th Street Bridge sometime around 1950 or so. The river ran straight away from the bridge, and it was "unquestionably" brown.[109] The river must have been carrying sewage that made the river that color. We cannot know whether Miller's vision of a badly polluted river is because hers is a decade later than that of Yalowitz and Raskin and the river had actually become dirtier or because she observed the river from a bridge under which the river is tidal (thus permitting observers to see both upstream and downstream sewage depending on whether the tide was ebbing or flowing).

By the late 1940s, plans were developed to construct the Hunts Point Water Treatment Plant. The drainage area for that plant included the lower Bronx River Watershed. The completion of the Hunts Point Water Treatment Plant in 1952 contributed to an improved quality of the river's water.

A watershed is a complex environment. A sewage plant may improve water quality while the building of a road may diminish water quality. To address increased use of the Bronx and Westchester County roads, road commissioner Robert Moses planned the extension and widening of the Bronx River Parkway southward into the Bronx. These improvements were completed in 1952.[110] As part of this construction, the river was further channeled and straightened. The Bronx River Parkway extension did not include a greenway buffer similar to that which was constructed farther north along the original Bronx River Parkway. This omission further exacerbated the eco-cultural divide between Bronx and Westchester County residents. The lower river suffered, as did the residents along its southern most reaches.

Chapter 6
Another Cleanup

The drastic decline of the Bronx after World War II has been well told elsewhere.[111] Roadways built under the Interstate Highway Act of 1956 facilitated the movement of more affluent residents out of the Bronx while dividing communities through which they were built. Landlords, in their pursuit of profit, mortgaged their buildings, stopped repairing them and cashed in on insurance payments when, during the 1970s, the Bronx burned. That decline negatively affected the Bronx River because there was increased dumping within the Bronx River Watershed. Social differences between the Bronx and Westchester County residents increased. In Westchester, the river with its green buffer running along almost its entire length continued to flourish, while the once majestic, small freshwater river in the Bronx became "hidden" behind small industry, apartment buildings, roads and junk. In 1999, a *New York Times* reporter, Barbara Stewart, expressed surprise that the "hidden" river was being discovered again: "It is not easy to hide a river. But except for wide, picturesque expanses in Westchester County and the Northern Bronx, especially in the New York Botanical Garden, the Bronx River is as unknown as an urban river can be. In the South Bronx, the waterway is hidden behind industrial buildings."[112]

The river's condition had not significantly changed in the immediate post–World War II period. It was still an open sewer and used as

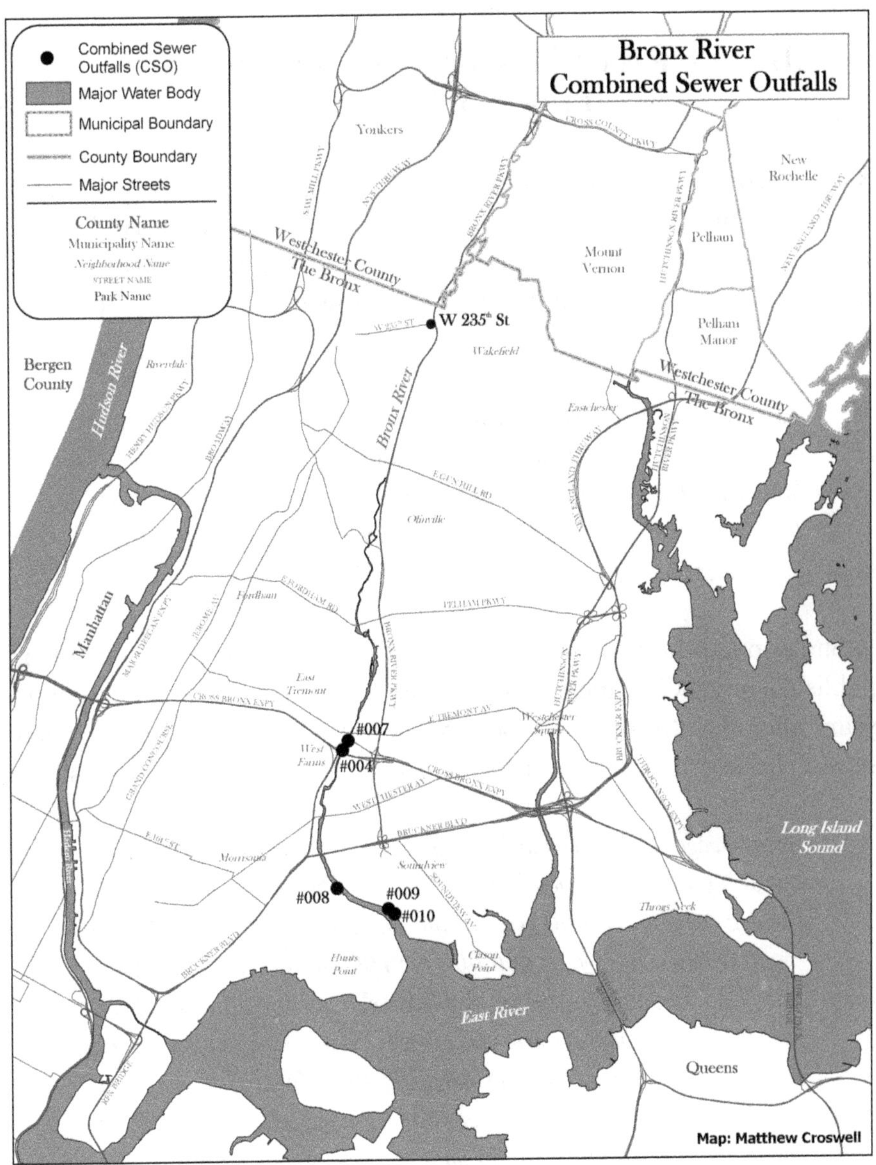

a garbage dump. What had changed from 1974 on was an amazing community effort in the Bronx to bring the river back to life. Distinct efforts by the Westchester community to clean up the river took place as well.

BRONX RIVER RESTORATION PUBLISHES THE THIRD BENCHMARK

Reclamation in the Bronx started in 1974 with the formation of Bronx River Restoration by local community residents. Ruth Anderberg spearheaded the organization and worked to clean up the West Farms reach of the Bronx River in the 1970s. Borrowing heavy equipment, she led a cleanup of

> *150 years' worth of refuse, from a turn-of-the-century wine press from one of the little French restaurants that closed 90 years ago, to hopelessly broken machines from a riverside appliance repair store* [as well as] *thousands of tires...* [and] *washing machines...a horse trailer*[,] *a piano soundboard*[,] *crankshafts*[,] *pieces of machinery and cars.*[113]

She also led the effort to create a *Master Plan* for the river. The plan, published in 1980, established a third benchmark for the river eighty-four years after the Bronx Valley Sewer Commission branded it an "open sewer." In describing the river's water quality, the *Master Plan* tells us:

> *Raw sewage which is emptied into the River at 235th and 233rd Streets causes a great deterioration in water quality. The maximum acceptable bacteria count of 10,000 per 100 milliliters of water is exceeded with counts climbing as high as 400,000 per 100 milliliters...Raw sewage leaks into* [the tidal zone of the River]*...as a result of overflows from the many combined storm and sanitary sewers, such as the one north of East 174th Street on the east bank of the River. In the East River both dissolved oxygen and coliform levels are substandard, and tidal action carries these waters upriver as far north as venue in West Farms.*[114]

Unfortunately, during heavy rains when the sewage treatment plants and the pipes leading to them cannot manage the increased volume of liquid, the overflows mentioned in the quotation above spew sewage into the river to this day. At 174th Street, there are two combined sewer overflows (CSOs), one on the east bank and the other one hundred feet downstream on the west bank. New York City labels these as CSO HP-007 and CSO HP-004.

The *Master Plan* is a benchmark in a second respect; it establishes a vision of what the Bronx River should look and smell like as an urban river from its source at the Kensico Dam to its mouth at the East River. The *Master Plan* envisioned a unified watershed that included both Westchester and the Bronx:

> *The success of a voluntary clean-up of the Bronx River at West Farms in the Bronx in 1974 was expressed in several ways. First was the emergence of this section of the River from a dismal throw-away place choked with debris into a sparkling stretch of free running water. The second was the consciousness-raising of neighborhood volunteers who came out of the experience with new insights into the value of an urban river and a new found sense of responsibility toward it. The River at this point has remained to all intents and purposes trash-free to this day. The third was the realization of the clean-up organizers that one cannot deal with a small section of a river and expect to make a permanent impact. This resulted in an investigation of the total River Corridor and the conclusion that the indivisible nature of the River as an ecosystem was the rationale for a systematic development of the River Basin from source to mouth.*[115]

The *Master Plan*'s vision is of the entire river, and of the river's watershed as well. The forward-looking plan envisioned a clean, swimmable river enhanced with bike and walkways along its banks. It also called for community participation in river cleanup, environmental education and clean-smelling, shaded river reaches. Community efforts to clean a river improve its environment, just as a cleaned river improves the quality of life for the community. Seeing these enhancements, community members are empowered to work for further change.

But the vision of a clean Bronx River with a greenway extending its entire length would not be achieved by the Bronx River Restoration or by the "15 to 20 groups working independently on the river."[116] The vision was subsequently adopted, however, by the Bronx River Restoration's successor organizations: the Bronx River Working Group and the Bronx River Alliance.

BRONX RIVER WORKING GROUP

The Bronx River Working Group (BRWG) formed in 1997[117] under the energetic leadership of Jenny Hoffner as coordinator and Majora Carter as its chairwoman. Hoffner was the knowledgeable outsider who never lived in the Bronx. Carter, a longtime, returned Bronx resident, was a strong, concerned community insider.

This was a stellar, inside-outside combination. Hoffner in 1997 joined New York City's Partnerships for Parks. One of her functions was to lead an effort to clean up the Bronx River, and as such she became the coordinator of the Bronx River Working Group. From the beginning, she saw her role in the reclamation of the Bronx River as an outsider. She planned to give it a few years and then leave.

> *It's true about my intent from the start to leave the project. As a catalyst project coordinator—and as an outsider—my role was to stir things up, focus the energy and put in place a structure through which work could continue. I never had any doubts that this was the right thing to do nor did I have any second thoughts. That isn't to say that I was not drawn to stay—because the truth is, it was the most exciting and compelling project on which I have ever worked. I love the Bronx River, the people and the work that we did—and all that you all still do!*[118]

That she would leave was not a hidden agenda. Hoffner made it clear to those around her that she saw her role as a "turnkey position." Her organization strategy was to pass leadership on to members of the community: "From the very beginning of the creation of the Bronx River Working Group, the coordinator's intention was to phase out her role after four years."[119] Part of her exit plan was to assemble a diverse group of people to plan for the river. She stayed as the coordinator for almost four years until just after the 2001 formation of the Bronx River Alliance.

The insider on the team was Majora Carter, who at that time was employed by the Point Community Development Corporation (The Point). Born in the Bronx, Carter was one of the many Bronx residents for whom the Bronx River was hidden. "As a child and as a young adult, living in the Bronx, I did not even know the river existed," Carter is fond of replying when asked about her Bronx River experience.[120] Carter's educational experience took her out of the Bronx for a number of years. It was not until she returned in 1997 that she discovered the Bronx River. With that revelation, Carter realized how important reclaiming the hidden, dumped in and degraded river would be for the communities surrounding it. By this time in her life, Carter had taken on a broad environmental consciousness in which reclaiming natural resources played a central role. She understood the Bronx River not only as a regional treasure but as a natural resource in dire need of, and worthy of, reclaiming.

Carter started working in the South Bronx and on Bronx River reclamation as a community organizer. The communities served by the Point were among the same communities that had been destroyed in the 1970s and were, by 1997, only beginning to come back to life. The Point was her full-time job. Her work as chairwoman of the Bronx River Working Group may have been part time, but it required, and got, a lot of her attention.

Hoffner and Carter joined forces with activists from other Bronx River neighborhoods. Alexie Torres-Fleming in 1994 founded Youth Ministries for Peace and Justice (YMPJ), becoming its executive director. Torres-Fleming was a long-term resident of the Bronx, growing up near to the Bronx River during the fires of the 1970s. She added a wide range of community contacts along with an articulate voice to the Bronx River Working Group effort. Dart Westphal, president of the Mosholu Preservation Corporation, a longtime Bronx activist, himself an articulate voice for community improvement, added a unique insight and an additional rich set of community contacts. Both Torres-Fleming and Westphal were to be chairpersons successively of the BRWG's successor organization.

Developing the BRWG's structure was an ongoing process. Funding was needed, events had to be planned, the organization's structure needed to be designed and a successor organization had to be established. Hoffner reports that there were no models to follow during the negotiations and design process that lead to creating the Bronx River Alliance:

> *I am not sure that I have other examples...The model the BRWG settled on for the structure of the Alliance was based on Prospect Park*

> *Alliance—but in that model* [the executive director] *stayed on and it wasn't community led...I don't remember having another model we were replicating. The certainty that we needed to phase ourselves out probably came from our partnership with National Park Service. Their model is to provide technical assistance and then phase their support out. I think that may have influenced the plan.*[121]

By gathering political support, several agencies began developing the coordination of work on and around the Bronx River, including the National Park Service, the Appalachian Mountain Club, New York City's Department of Parks and Recreation, the New York City Parks Foundation and the Partnership for Parks. The BRWG's meetings were also supported, explicitly or implicitly, by the employers of those attending the meetings (salaries continued to be paid while individual participants attended the group's meetings) and by volunteer attendees.

The Golden Ball, just like everyone else, had to portage around mill dams. In the background is the Bolton Dam in the middle of the Bronx Zoo. The Golden Ball, an event intended to bring recognition to the Bronx River, no longer takes place. With the increased funding and attention to river improvements and with the river increasingly having come out of hiding, other priorities have taken precedence. *Photo by Bronx River Alliance.*

As part of their newly found, coordinated pride in their community and in New York City's only freshwater river, the BRWG initiated what became annual Bronx-based celebrations of the river. The first of these, in 1999, was "the Golden Ball," intended to be a day of canoe trips down the river, events on the banks of the river and, in general, a day of celebrating what the river was and could become. The event's focus was a large floating golden ball that canoeists followed down the river. The celebration included dancers on the shore at various places. Passersby on the shore began to recognize the recreational possibilities of a cleaned-up Bronx River. The event symbolized the unified and coordinated activities of, by then, the more than thirty-five government agencies, community groups (both local and regional) and individual community members[122] in cleaning up and improving the Bronx River as a recreational resource and community amenity.

The Bronx River Working Group developed the genesis of four directions of Bronx River improvements: ecology, education, greenway and outreach. Ecological restoration had been a prime objective of the 1980 *Master Plan*. The BRWG, and later the Bronx River Alliance, adopted this focus by planning for environmental investigation, clean up, erosion and storm water control. For all this, significant additional funding was needed. Both the BRWG and the alliance pursued funding sources.

Education, one of the functions of the Bronx River Restoration, remained a focus for the BRWG. People in nearby neighborhoods needed to learn about the river. Local students can become informed about the river through environmental studies in schools.[123] Teachers and students can have hands-on experiences with nature by taking the classroom into the field. For example, students can test for dissolved oxygen and pH levels in the river and learn about environmental issues. While education does not need as much funding as capital projects, financial support for in-the-field education programs is a continuing need.

The vision of a twenty-three-mile greenway stretching from the mouth of the Bronx River at the East River to the Kensico Dam was also coming into sharp relief. Here, too, planning and funding would be required. Overarching all this was a vision of community involvement in cleaning up and revealing a previously hidden river. A vision of a

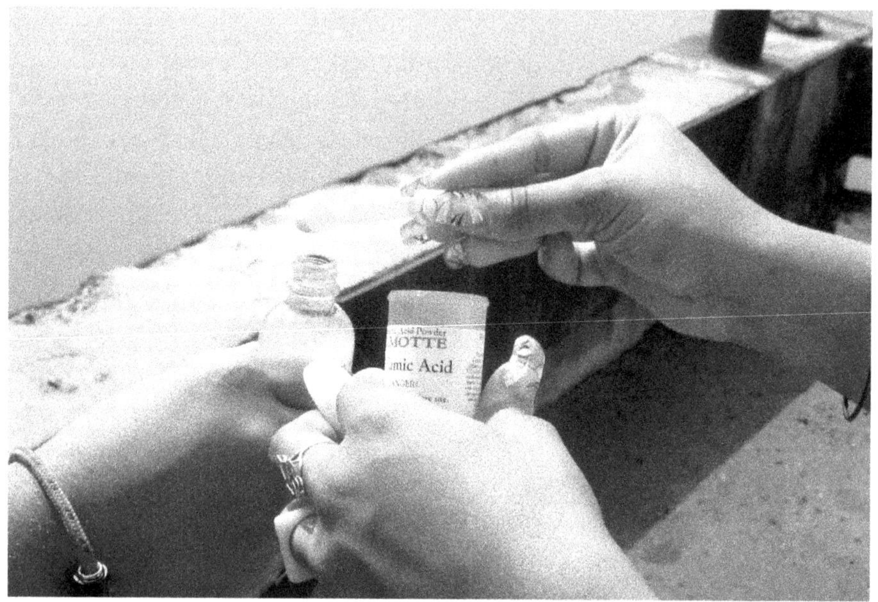

Student fieldwork at the Bronx River requires a school to have willing teachers, administrative support and funding for chemical kits. Students receive an out-of-classroom experience in environmental science and policy that leaves a lasting impression. Here students are testing the Bronx River Estuary running by Concrete Plant Park between Westchester Avenue and Bruckner Boulevard. *Photo by Maarten de Kadt.*

bottom up, grass-roots political advocacy structure came into focus. The need for planning community events and for continuous outreach became ever clearer.

Just before it completed its transformation into its successor organization—the Bronx River Alliance—the Bronx River Working Group grew to sixty-five government, nongovernment and community participants. After decades of struggle, the stage finally was set for significant reclamation of the Bronx River.

Chapter 7

The Amazing Bronx River Cleanup

The cleanup of the Bronx River that spanned between 1974, when Bronx River Restoration was formed, and 2001, when the Bronx River Working Group ended its short reign, was only a prelude to the cleanup efforts in the first decade of the twenty-first century. Numerous car bodies—among other debris—contaminated the southern reaches of the Bronx River. Everywhere pipes ejecting contaminated effluent burdened the river. Continued river cleanup not only required significant amounts of money (most likely to come from federal, state and city agencies), it also required increased enforcement of antidumping laws to prevent additional dumping. This increase in enforcement, in turn, required stepped-up coordination among the various community groups and government agencies involved in the cleanup effort.

Bronx River Alliance

The community organizations working to clean up the Bronx River were composed of citizens most familiar with the river's actual condition. This unique melding of governmental organizations and local community activists fostered improvements that have set a national standard for the reclamation of urban rivers. One such group (navigating between the desires of the community organizations and the Department of Parks and Recreation) has been the Bronx River Alliance.

From the very beginning, the Bronx River Alliance focused on reclaiming a natural resource: the Bronx River and its watershed. The Mission Statement of the Bronx River Alliance set a tone of cooperation and environmental reclamation:

> *The Bronx River Alliance serves as a coordinated voice for the river and works in harmonious partnership to protect, improve and restore the Bronx River corridor and greenway so that they can be healthy ecological, recreational, educational and economic resources for the communities through which the river flows.*[124]

The alliance also focused on community building. In a world comprised of large institutions, corporations and governments, the Bronx River Alliance's designers had the goal of creating an organically democratic institution. From its inception, the alliance's governing structure was unusual, not only because its originating organization phased itself out but also because its board of directors, an amalgam of public and private participants, included members of the community which it served. The original framework was meant to be bottom up and democratic. It included four teams, each headed by a chair and a cochair. In addition to the teams, the organization's structure had a management and a field staff led by an executive director and a board of directors. The board of directors included officers, members-at-large and the chair and cochair of each of the teams. The executive director attends board of directors' meetings but does not have a vote. Since the teams were largely composed of community members, the thinking went that the board of directors would therefore be comprised of community members. By 2011, this structure has changed slightly. Now there are only three teams. Formerly, the team cochairs became members of the board. Now several choose not to do so. In addition, staff and volunteers come to the alliance from locations outside of the watershed.

The alliance was constrained by its dual organization structure. On the one hand it was focused on community input. On the other hand, major decisions and initiatives had to be approved by the Department of

Parks and Recreation. Thus the alliance's structure violated a traditional management concept of maintaining a single line of control. Here there was a dual management structure: government and community. This dichotomy has played out behind the scenes.

Keeping the dual organization structure in mind, the Bronx River Alliance focused on involving the community it served in the day-to-day decision making, thus inserting elements of democratic participation and of civic engagement in the economic choices being made about the river and its watershed. This feature is difficult to maintain in our society where economic decision making is generally controlled by business and government. Rarely do communities participate so directly in economic choices as they did here. This was an organic, homegrown excursion in the direction of economic democracy by the founders of the Bronx River Alliance.[125]

The bottom-up nature of the new Bronx River Alliance engendered excitement in its participants. Clearly something unusual was happening. The alliance understood that it would have to work to maintain the vitality of and the continued participation in this form of decision making that could be easily overpowered by the more usual, undemocratic economic decision making dominating on the national, state and city levels. I was caught up in my own participation in the alliance. While a volunteer to alliance activities, I was hard at work with my students. One of my school projects was to involve students in learning about the history and ecology of the river, but that was not my only class. I was empowered, however, by my participation with the Bronx River Alliance's concern for the environment. And I was largely unaware of the role being played by the Department of Parks and Recreation. While I saw department personnel at river events, I was unaware that a complex set of decisions were constantly being made.

Since the Bronx River Alliance's 2001 formation, activity along the Bronx River and participation in various improvement projects have dramatically increased. Parks have been opened, erosion control has been implemented, flood plains have been reestablished, education programs have been ongoing and there have been multiple evaluations of the river's environment. The work of river restoration is both physical and political. Included in the twenty-member staff, there are ten interns a year, twenty-five regularly active volunteers (though there are many more during the course of a year) and a fifteen-member board of directors, all focused on the physical reclamation of the Bronx River; there is also the Conservation Crew, varying in size from five to ten members. It does the hands-on work of river improvement. The crew keeps the river navigable by removing natural and human-made obstacles. It performs erosion control, as well as removes invasive plants. The crew cleans up litter; plants trees, shrubs and plants; and develops park land. The Bronx River Alliance reports:

> *From 2006–2007, together with hundreds of volunteers, the Conservation Crew freed the river's waters of an astonishing amount of debris: over 3,000 tires, 7,500 other large objects, and some 85 tons of litter and flotsam. In addition, the Conservation Crew has also planted over 15,000 trees, and reclaimed more than 60 acres of parkland along the Bronx River since 2005.*[126]

Crew members are recruited from the local communities along the river and more widely from the city at large. The crew provides field training to various community groups. In addition to their hands-on experience, crew members work with community-based organizations, school groups and other river volunteers. With their outdoor forestry, river experience and their leadership role with volunteer workers, members of the crew gain experience that enables them to move on to careers in ecology and team management. Several have become long-term employees. Another byproduct of the alliance's work is to provide jobs to diverse populations, while serving as a catalyst for community regeneration.

After the first ten years, the alliance's executive director, Linda Cox, believes its greatest accomplishment has been "staying true to our mission. We pride ourselves on our transparency. The community knows what we are doing. We focus on getting input from and keeping communities informed. I've been told 'the river looks cleaner.' And it does even though I know sewage waste remains a problem."[127] "Staying true to our mission" has included arranging for and enforcing appropriate antidumping laws along the river. This was largely a Department of

An abandoned concrete plant at Westchester Avenue was notorious for being a convenient dumping site. It was relatively isolated, so no one would notice illegal dumping. It had a paved road, providing easy access. By April 2002, cleanup was well underway. The cement blocks in the foreground, placed only a few months before, were painted bright colors by a local school group. Increased enforcement, the concrete block barrier and increased use of the site, by then owned by the Department of Parks and Recreation, virtually eliminated dumping at that location. *Photo by Maarten de Kadt.*

Parks and Recreation function. Cox understands that reclaiming the Bronx River (or any river for that matter) requires continued enforcement. In the early years of the twenty-first century, preventing further dumping into the Bronx River was urgently required. By 2002, to prevent dumping, heavy concrete cubes were placed at strategic locations along the Bronx River to create a barrier. No longer would it be easy to drive trucks to the edge of the river and dump tires or cars into the river to avoid paying fees for proper disposal.

More recently, success has led to a new challenge: beavers have returned to the Bronx River, reflecting the improved environment, but they girdle trees, causing them to die and either remain standing or topple, sometimes into the river. These beaver-damaged trees can affect the environment in three ways: first, unsightly standing dead trees are not pleasing to local residents using Bronx River forests for

Signs of returned beavers to the Bronx River abound, but felled trees may block the river. If the navigation channel is to be maintained, these logs need to be cleared. Without the need for navigation, trees in the river would collect debris and might even form the basic structure for beaver dams. *Photo by Bronx River Alliance.*

recreation; second, loss of the trees means a loss of important erosion protection that living trees provide; and third, actual blockage of the river often means one tree collects other floating debris or perhaps even a whole beaver dam. When those trees block the river, they need to be removed if the purpose is to keep the river navigable. Of course, beavers are not the only cause of falling trees; storms cause their share of damage too.

From 2001 to 2011, the alliance's accomplishments are impressive.[128] Table 5 summarizes its achievements but doesn't really do justice to the alliance's profound impacts on the river and nearby communities. The alliance's successes include the removal of major obstacles, planting trees and shrubs, installing erosion controls, publishing plans, guides and educational materials and opening five public parks.

Table 5: Reclaiming the Bronx River: 2001–11 by the Bronx River Alliance and Its Partners

- Removed river obstacles:
  26 cars (63 between 1997 and 2001)
  6 motorcycles
  145 full river blockages (27 between 1997 and 2001)
  317 tons of garbage (340 between 1997 and 2001)
  27,000 cubic yards of invasive vegetation
  6,730 tires (20,230 between 1997 and 2001)
  8,494 other large objects
- Planted 84,725 trees, shrubs and grasses (20,525 between 1997 and 2001)
- Installed shoreline control and stabilization and erosion control along Shoelace Park
- Renovated and opened parks:
  Muskrat Cove
  Hunts Point Riverside Park
  Concrete Plant Park at Westchester Avenue
  West Farms Rapids
  Starlight Park
  Soundview Park waterfront improvements
  Shoelace Park improvements:
    - 211th St entrance
    - 219th St entrance including a rain garden with a 6000 gallon underground storm water retention tank
    - 222nd St entrance
    - Pathway improvements at northern end of the park including a small rain garden
- Built 4 new access points to the river (2 prior to 2001)
- Installed about 350 storm drain markers
- Installed 9 rain water harvesting burials (a storm water capture method)
- Founding member and active participant in SWIM (Storm Water Infrastructure Matters), a New York City wide coalition looking for solutions to the city's combined sewer overflows

- Published:
  Bronx River Watershed Intermunicipal Watershed Management Plan (2011)
  Bronx River Paddling Guide (2010)
  Shoelace Park Master Plan (2010)
  Bronx River Classroom: The Inside Track for Educators (2007)
  Bronx River Walking Guide (2006)
  The Bronx River Greenway Plan (2005)
  The Bronx River Ecological Restoration And Management Plan (2005)
  Bronx River Map & Guide (1998, 2003, 2007)

(Bronx River Alliance with the help of Maggie Greenfield as of April 2011)

FIVE PARKS

The stories of five Bronx parks—Riverside Park, Concrete Plant Park, Bronx River Rapids Park, Starlight Park and Shoelace Park—are but examples of the physical makeover occurring on and around the Bronx River. These parks are significant, as they offer nearby communities amenities, improving residents' quality of life by providing open spaces for recreation and relaxation in an otherwise crowded urban environment. In addition, as part of a larger greenway, they provide environmental buffers around the river, improving water quality.

Hunts Point Riverside Park

By the late 1990s, an abandoned sliver of land squeezed between the Hunts Point Food Market and a functioning scrap yard at the end of Lafayette Avenue, just past Edgewater Road, provided limited access to the Bronx River for the local community. There, students and residents could fish using seine nets or fishing rods and, in so doing, see the abundance of life in the Bronx River estuary. Regrettably, these participants also got to see an abundance of drug paraphernalia dumped on the abandoned property.

The Partnership for Parks', the Bronx River Working Group's and later the alliance's vision for this sliver of land in a densely populated, industrial

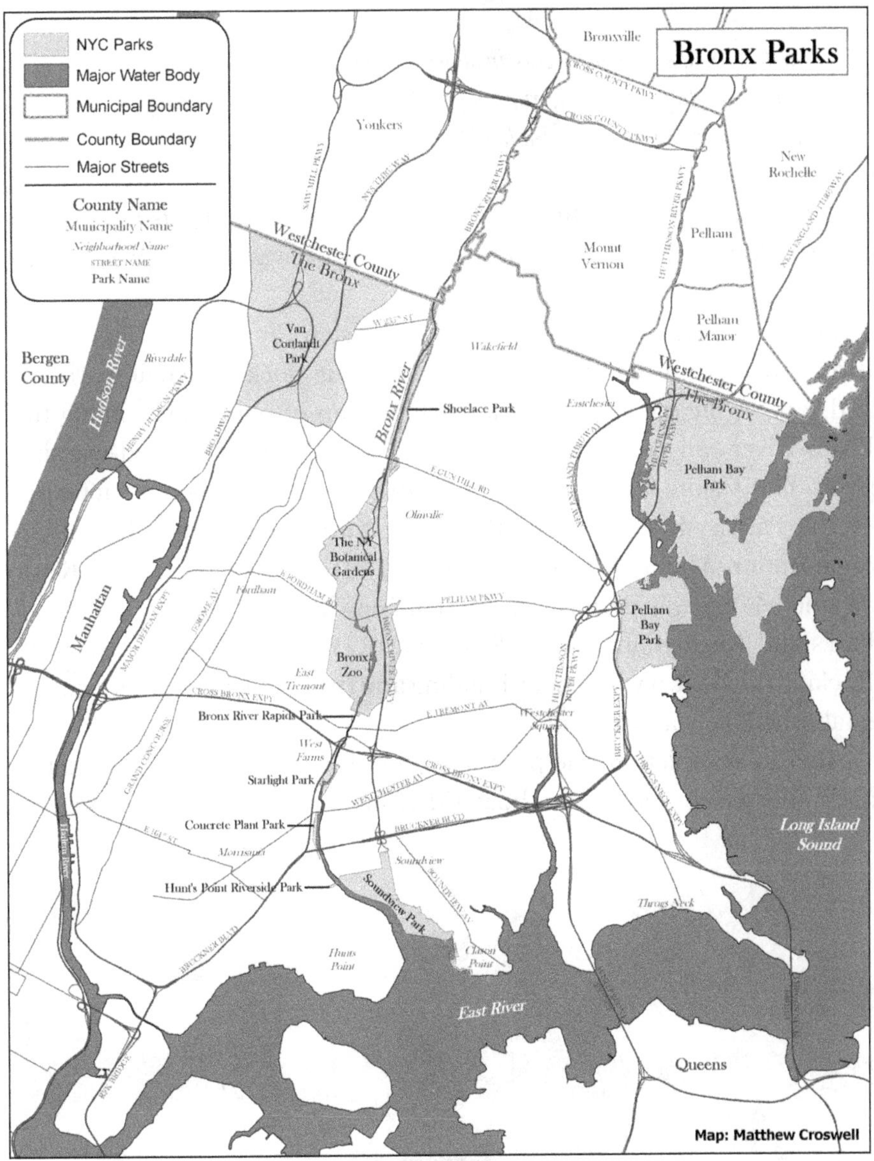

and underserved community, was a riverside park. Central to formulating this park was active community participation in the design process:

> *At one point, the design team hung a banner on the site showing the preliminary plan, with post-it notes so that residents could attach comments and suggestions. For the Parks Department landscape*

> *architects, the design process included getting to know the site form the land and from the river, running scoping meetings, and meeting with community organization leaders.*[129]

One outcome of this inclusive design process was the Hunts Point Food Market donation of an important triangle of waterfront property to the park.

The proposed project included the provision for public access to the Bronx River with the installation of a floating dock for small rowboats and canoes, the completion of a small portion of a greenway along the Bronx River and a careful design for a small but beautiful, award-winning park. The vision was achieved through sustained grass-roots activities by the Partnership for Parks, the Point, Sustainable South Bronx (an organization Majora Carter formed in 2001) and by the Bronx River Alliance. Work was performed through New York City's Department of Parks and Recreation with $3.2 million in city funding. Adjacent to it, Rocking the Boat, a youth boat-building and river education organization, established its headquarters.

After its completion, the park has been the site of festivals, weddings and other celebrations, free boat rides, lunchtime activities for nearby

Hunts Point Riverside Park, on the west side of the Bronx River Estuary, replaced an empty lot at the end of Lafayette Avenue, replete with debris including used drug paraphernalia. The fence in the background at right marks the park boundary to the Hunts Point Food Market. The apartment buildings in the background left of center are on the eastern side of the Bronx River Estuary. *Photo by George Bloomer, RLA, New York City Department of Parks and Recreation, for the Bronx River Alliance.*

workers, a play space for local children and other leisure activities. The park's various plantings give one indication of the park's success: "The [park's] designers report that there has been very little plant replacement since the opening, suggesting that the plants have thrived and that there has been little damage inflicted by users. They comment, 'It's obvious that the community cares, because it's maintained well.'"[130] Undoubtedly, Hunts Point Riverside Park contributes to an increased quality of life for the local community and businesses.[131]

Concrete Plant Park

A seven-acre site between Bruckner Boulevard and Westchester Avenue was used by a concrete company until 1987, when the company failed. The site was also used as the home base of the *Bronx Queen*, an excursion boat serving the Hunts Point and West Farms communities until December 2, 1989, when it hit an underwater obstacle and sank. After the property was abandoned, it became a tire dump. By 2000, the land was actively being considered for a roadway to access the Hunts Point Food Market in order to remove large trucks from residential Hunts Point streets. In that year, the New York City Department of Parks and Recreation acquired the site.[132]

With its acquisition by the department, the possibility that the land would be used as a roadway diminished, but it was not eliminated. Several years of struggle among community organizations and state agencies ensued. The city had to be persuaded not to sell the land to a private developer. Primary players in the struggle were Youth Ministries for Peace and Justice, the state's Department of Transportation, the Bronx River Working Group, followed by the Bronx River Alliance and the city's Department of Parks and Recreation. Designs for the abandoned property included only a roadway, only a park, some combination of the two and whatever the plans of the potential private developers were. Community meetings were held. With support from the Department of Parks and Recreation and good organizing by Youth Ministries for Peace and Justice, the city retained ownership of the land. The park-only plan won out. Construction on the project began in 2006.[133]

Rehabilitation of the land required the removal of more than twenty-one thousand tires from mudflats exposed at low tide. Homeless families that had built sheds under the trees along the riverbank also had to be relocated (much as families living south of the 174th Street Bridge in 1948 had to be removed for the creation of the new Starlight Park—discussed in the next section). Also relocated were two, otherwise homeless, "caretakers" of the abandoned site. Their relocation was required before reconstruction could begin. Success in finding suitable housing for them was accomplished by two Youth Ministries for Peace and Justice activists, David Shuffler and Henry Lajara. "I occasionally see [the former caretakers] on the street and say hi," Shuffler reports.[134]

Cordgrass (*Spartina alterniflora*) was planted along the riverbank by the New York City Department of Parks and Recreation's Natural Resources Group, assisted by the Bronx River Alliance's Conservation Crew, in the hope that it would provide bird and aquatic habitat and water filtering. With too low a salt level, the spartina failed. Nature replaced it with water hemp. This plant with its rich supply of berries, loved by songbirds, stands in place of the spartina.

The design of a park and its construction had to be arranged and funding had to be found and allocated. According to the Bronx River

The *Bronx Queen* at her pier circa 1980. In the background is the then functioning concrete plant at Westchester Avenue. After serving its community for many years, the excursion boat ran aground and sank off Breezy Point in 1989. *Bronx River Restoration,* Master Plan.

Concrete is an important building component in urban development. Transit-Mix Concrete, circa 1980, functioned just south of the *Bronx Queen* pier. *Bronx River Restoration,* Master Plan.

Remnants of the *Bronx Queen*'s pier circa 2004 at high tide just south of Westchester Avenue. *Photo by Maarten de Kadt.*

Transit-Mix Concrete went out of business in 1987. By 1999, its facility was a rusting, dangerous hulk on the banks of the Bronx River. Several of these structures were preserved to maintain the historic quality of what became a park. In the background on the right is the elevated train bridge crossing the Bronx River at Westchester Avenue. *Photo by Maarten de Kadt.*

Transit-Mix Concrete's corporate sign (now vanished) gave researchers and local residents a clue to the identity of the previous owner of the property at Westchester Avenue. *Photo by Maarten de Kadt.*

This view from the abandoned Concrete Plant site shows that even in the worst of times the Bronx River's prospects are obvious. The distinct shape of the Westchester Avenue train bridge is in the background. *Photo by Maarten de Kadt.*

In 2003, New York City's Natural Resources Group (a division of the Department of Parks and Recreation) planted cordgrass on the bank of the abandoned concrete plant as part of its river cleanup effort. Today, water hemp is thriving here. *Photo by Maarten de Kadt.*

There were more than twenty-one thousand tires to remove from this mud flat. In the background is the remaining *Bronx Queen* pier. *Photo by Maarten de Kadt.*

By 2002, the removal of thousands of tires from the Bronx River was underway. These tires are piled up in what became Concrete Plant Park. The task would take several years. *Photo by Maarten de Kadt.*

Concrete blocks to prevent additional dumping eventually would take their place on the road where these tiers sat in 2002. *Photo by Maarten de Kadt.*

More than seventy car bodies, both in the river and on the river's bank, were removed by the New York National Guard, most before 2002. *Photo by Bronx River Alliance.*

Left: The hard work of these National Guard personnel leaves no doubt that many cars were removed. *Photo by Jenny Hoffner.*

Below: In this very urban setting, the original structures of the defunct concrete plant stand unmoved in the new park. Here the Bronx River Estuary ebbs and flows in its most urban setting. In the foreground is Amtrak's main line New York City to Boston, originally built in 1873 by New York, New Haven & Hartford Railroad. *Photo by Maarten de Kadt.*

Alliance's announcement of the ribbon cutting event, $11.4 million in funding came from Mayor Michael R. Bloomberg, Congressman José E. Serrano, the Bronx Borough president's office,[135] a Recreation Trails Grant from the New York State Office of Parks, Recreation and Historic Preservation and mitigation funds from the construction of the Croton Water Filtration Plant. On October 30, 2009, ten years after the site became Department of Parks and Recreation's property, the Bronx River Alliance and the department celebrated the opening of Concrete Plant Park as an additional jewel for the local community.

Starlight Park

The fifteen-acre Starlight Park, named after the amusement park of the 1930s that was located north and east of this location, lies on the western bank of the Bronx River south of the 174th Street Bridge. It is sandwiched between the Sheridan Expressway and the Bronx River. Before it was identified as a park in need of renovation and as the future headquarters of the Bronx River Alliance, it served as the home baseball field for local schools and community organizations.[136] Early in the renovation process, remains of the operation of the manufactured gas plant (MGP), discussed in Chapter 3, were uncovered: "The initial analytical data suggests that sediment of the Bronx River may contain elevated background concentrations of metals, however, significant impacts associated with the former MGP operations were not identified."[137] Community pressure, activism and political pressure to assure thorough cleanup of this brownfield site before building a park on it was spearheaded by Youth Ministries for Peace and Justice. In response, cleanup teams increased the final addition of top soil used to complete the remediation of the Manufactured Gas Plant site from an originally planned three feet to a more protective six feet, thereby encapsulating whatever danger remained following removal of contaminated soil.[138] In 2010, David Shuffler, at thirty-one years of age, took over the executive directorship of YMPJ.

Shuffler started working on the river's cleanup during his teenage years. Today he is central to promoting the mission statement neatly written on a display board in YMPJ's main room: "To rebuild the neighborhood of the Bronx River and Soundview/Bruckner by preparing young people to become prophetic voices for peace and justice." He is thoughtful about his task. His passion is to empower young people. This is part of his own "give back," as he feels he was empowered during his cleanup days. He knows getting active community involvement is difficult. He is aware that his meteoric rise to executive director is unusual. In these difficult economic times, YMPJ is smaller in size and program offering than it was just a few years ago. But it is still serving neighborhood youth "through political education, spiritual formation, and youth and community development and organizing." To keep the pressure on for river improvement, Shuffler realizes YMPJ cannot do it alone. Needed is the help of unaffiliated community members. Community members' participation in economic decision making has been uneven for at least two reasons: first, residents in this underserved, economically challenged

David Shuffler as a youth participating in a river cleanup activity. *Photo by Youth Ministries for Peace and Justice.*

community continue to face their own personal economic obstacles, and second, the effect of participation in river and community cleanup on residents' own lives is often not obvious to them. Nevertheless, Shuffler feels he has "the pulse of the community."[139]

As a fine-tuned grass-roots organizer, Shuffler walks neighborhood streets, "talks with folks and listens to them." He remains concerned with environmental justice issues just as he was more than ten years ago when he began discussing the contrast of the dumped-on lower Bronx River to the much more bucolic upper reaches of the river in more affluent neighborhoods. Today, YMPJ continues to work for the decommissioning of the nearby Sheridan Expressway that runs along the west side of the Bronx River so that it can be replaced by affordable housing and parks needed by this underserved community. Shuffler is a much needed community activist deeply concerned with both the environmental and economic well-being of his neighbors.

Now that the topsoil is in place, the reconstruction of Starlight Park—the park that long has been a focus of YMPJ's (and Shuffler's)

A footbridge, new in 2011, will enable hikers and bicyclists to cross the Bronx River in the West Farms area just north of the 174th Street Bridge without resorting to city streets. *Photo by Maarten de Kadt.*

efforts—is finally underway. "Did you see the foot bridge just placed over the Bronx River connecting Starlight Park to the Bronx River Greenway?" Shuffler asked. When completed around 2012, the park will have waterfront access, a floating dock, a comfort station and a boathouse with a classroom and offices for the Bronx River Alliance. It too offers waterfront amenities that improve the quality of life for the local community.

West Farms Rapids Park

West Farms, the community around this gorgeous park, was settled in 1664 by English farmers moving into a Dutch territory. They named it West Farms because it was located west of their original farms near what is now Westchester Square in the Bronx. The township of West Farms was incorporated in 1846. Today, the area is one of the economically poorest in the Bronx. The rapids flowing by this park compose one of the narrower and faster flowing parts of the Bronx River. The park is situated just north of the transition point where the river becomes an estuary (that part of a river affected by the ocean's tides). North of the transition point the river is a freshwater river. South of the transition point the river contains ocean salt.

Almost thirty-seven years after Ruth Anderberg led the Bronx River Restoration in its cleaning of the West Farms section of the Bronx River, the park has been renovated. The park will afford better river access along a stretch of the river that has long been hidden, neglected and dangerous and has fostered drug use and prostitution. The area has been cleaned up and made more accessible. The new park includes a boat launch, an especially useful addition because water flows rapidly at this part of the river. Canoeists who have had the unfortunate experience of capsizing their canoes will have an easier time pulling their narrow boats out of the river. Other paddlers, wanting to avoid going around upstream portages, will have easier access to the river using this park's boat launch. This shady, renovated park, opening in 2011, enhances the quality of life of the nearby residents.

Shoelace Park

Since 1999, Shoelace Park, which stretches from 211th to 231st Streets, has been the starting point of the Amazing Bronx River Flotilla, a yearly celebration of the resurgence of the Bronx River. At the 219th Street boat launch, members of the Bronx River Alliance's Conservation Crew, staff and a lot of volunteers assist some two hundred participants into about one hundred canoes provided by the Department of Parks and Recreation. This event highlights another of the crew's functions: it transports canoes to the launch site, removes the canoes from the river at three different points to portage around dams and finally collects and returns the equipment to the department's storage places.

Shoelace Park's improvements over the years include improving entrance ways, greenway connections, storm water management, ecological maintenance, as well as riparian invasive species management.[140] Erosion along the shore of the Bronx River has been a problem. The straightening of the river, with the building of the railroads and the

In April 2002, stakes were used to hold the coir logs in place along the Shoelace Park channel. Today the stakes and the coir logs have become an almost hidden part of the river's edge. *Photo by Maarten de Kadt.*

parkway, created the problem of shoreline erosion. Erosion possibilities are enhanced by the faster movement of a straightened river and by the removal of trees and shrubs that result when a river's course is altered. During the 1950s, Robert Moses reconstructed the parkway on the western side of the river but did not include riverbank erosion measures. By 2002, the Bronx River Alliance's Conservation Crew had installed a series of biologs (coconut fiber rolled into a tubelike, biodegradable, "coir net log") along the unprotected side of the Bronx River Shoelace channel. The early twenty-first-century riverbank improvement effort seems successful as each year the river's bank, in this reach of the river, appears more stable.

WESTCHESTER

The Bronx River Parkway Reservation is the northern-most significant park along the river. The Westchester County government owns and maintains the Bronx River Parkway, the pathway along the river and the parkland that was created when the road was built. Community groups and the county government come together through the work of the Bronx River Parkway Reservation Conservancy, which acts as a unifying force on the Bronx River in Westchester County.

In addition to the activity of local government and the conservancy, several community organizations pay attention to their own section of the Bronx River. One such organization is the Garrett Park Neighborhood Association (GPNA), a regular neighborhood association of fourteen independent apartment buildings in Yonkers. GPNA has essentially adopted a short section of the river. Westchester is fortunate to have organizations like these that pay special attention to small sections of the river. Numerous functions, sponsored by the county, are held along the river, including the occasional closing of the parkway to provide recreation for residents in the form of bicycle events, recreational biking, road races and more.

Attention is being paid to the health of the river. There is an annual river cleanup: Pitch in for Parks. Local groups take responsibility to clean sections of the river. Vine cutters are actively removing invasive vines from trees in the park. Combined sewer and storm water drainage systems continue to exist and require attention as they do in the lower reaches of the river. In Westchester, floods remain an issue, as the watershed has been largely developed. Impervious surfaces lead to the ready flooding of the Bronx River. In addition, there are a number of current capital projects: the Bronxville Lake is undergoing extensive redesign along with riverbank stabilization; the Hartsdale to Scarsdale Path is being planned along the river; the Scarsdale Dam has been rebuilt, and there are plans to replace the bridge at that point; Garth Wood is undergoing renovation; and all along the river there are replanting and cleaning projects. The many separate organizations and community groups contribute to public activities along the northern reaches of the river. With the completion of the Bronx River Parkway in 1925, this portion of the river has been more parklike in nature. The Westchester County portion of the Bronx River benefits from the environmental condition of its watershed: a healthy watershed results in a healthy water body at its bottom. That is the case here. Even though the urgency of cleanup is not as great as the urban portion in the Bronx, Westchester section of the Bronx River benefits from the constant attention of its nearby communities.[141]

Community Involvement

A watershed and the population living in it are a complex social, economic and environmental network in which the individual parts affect the whole. The river and its nearby residential communities are interdependent. A clean river is integral to the watershed through which it flows, just as healthy watersheds result in a healthy water body at its bottom. Both cocreate a healthy community. Reclaiming natural resources through grass-roots organizing and applications of economic democracy benefits the immediate community and beyond.

Community activism, starting with the work of the Bronx River Restoration in 1974 and extending through the work of the Bronx River Alliance, has led to broad-based funding of Bronx River improvements. These monies have been steadily increasing (see Table 6).

Table 6: Number of Bronx River Alliance and Bronx River Working Group Partners and Financial Supporters

Year*	1998	2000	2004	2005	2008
Community-based organizations			19	19	**
Nongovernmental organization			24	33	58
Federal government			9	8	5
State and local governments			16	24	21
Schools			20	24	32
Financial Supporters***			27	28	58
Total	**35**	**65**	**115**	**136**	**174**

* 1998 and 2000 individual breakdowns not given. See Carrie Grassi.

** Included with NGOs.

*** Not including individual donors.

(Bronx River Alliance, Annual Reports 2004, 2005 and 2008 and Grassi, "The Development of the Bronx River Alliance")

As a result of all of this, the environment of the Bronx River has improved much to the satisfaction of those who, over the past many years, have worked hard to attain that end. South Bronx activist Alexie Torres-Fleming explains:

> *Over the past ten years we have struggled to reclaim the river. The river has had* [70] *cars and* [21,000] *tires removed from it. The site of the concrete plant* [has been] *made into a waterfront park. The $11 million that had been planned for a truck route nearby is going to be used to create a greenway up and down the river. We struggled with our local energy company to arrange an appropriate cleanup—we got all the*

> *contamination removed, the ground water treated, and six feet of clean soil above it. The park will now have new access points. One seven-acre park opened last month, and a second will open in 2012.*[142]

The twenty-first-century removal of river obstructions is reminiscent of the removal of debris by the Bronx Parkway Commission early during the twentieth century. With the significant improvement of the river's environment, with the removal of illegally dumped cars, tires, appliances and more and with the planting of trees, the creation of parks, the increase of recreation on the river, paradoxically, a new worry arises. Will the environmental enhancements and the increase in property values near the river cause gentrification and, along with it, the displacement of long-established residents?

A test case in this matter is playing out in West Farms real estate adjacent to the river. Since April 2010, New York City's Department of City Planning has been considering a rezoning proposal for this area. A developer proposes to change a manufacturing zone in West Farms to a residential zone to facilitate the building of new residences. This kind of proposal would only have occurred because the Bronx River's environment has greatly improved. No matter what the resolution of the rezoning application, the issues raised by the West Farms proposal concern the health of the watershed and those who live in it. The Bronx River Alliance has raised a number of concerns about the proposal. How will these buildings affect the greenway being constructed along the entire length of the Bronx River? What will happen to open space? Will the developer support maintenance of the river and its greenway both financially and with the help of its own employees? How will sewage and storm water management be affected? Will there be sufficient affordable housing? Will existing rent remain stable for long-term residents? Will local schools become overcrowded as a result of new residential construction? What will happen to the jobs and the workers that hold them within the existing manufacturing zone? What will happen to the contiguous residential neighborhoods if this development moves forward?[143] As with any rezoning proposal, this one will require an environmental impact statement that will examine these issues and, importantly, give the community an opportunity to express its own vision for the area.

Improvements, on and around the Bronx River, resulted from the efforts of local residents. They should receive the benefit too. Their displacement would be an unintended and unacceptable result of river improvement. Increased real estate values, along with associated higher rent, should not force long-term residents to move away from the community that they have helped to clean up.

Chapter 8

Reclaiming a Natural Resource

Natural resources are imperiled worldwide. Oil spills jeopardize fisheries and beaches. Nuclear plant meltdowns in the United States, in Russia and in Japan have contaminated people, farmland and threaten water bodies. Cutting off mountain tops to mine coal affects the water quality of nearby rivers and streams. Improper waste disposal, both industrial and residential, contaminates nearby groundwater. Hydraulic fracturing (hydrofracking) in pursuit of unlocking vast reserves of natural gas has also caused severe damage to drinking water supplies. Industrial farming methods have degraded the quality of the land. Each one of these actions have been taken by individual corporations and condoned by governments. The communities involved suffered.

The Bronx River, until very recently, has been used without regard to socio-environmental consequences. The river's use over four hundred years has enriched and continues enriching the lives of people residing in its watershed and beyond. On the other hand, its abuse has resulted in the river's degradation and a decline of the quality of life for those living near it. Its degradation was fostered by the mill and industry owners using the river as a resource and government bodies ignorant of the consequences or unwilling or unable to promulgate or enforce environmental regulations. Reclaiming the Bronx River (as is the reclaiming of most degraded natural resources) is a daunting, and in at least in one respect, an impossible task. The Bronx River is coming back as an enhancement to the quality of life of communities around it. However, the river is not likely to serve as a source of drinking water any time in the near future. We can reclaim it, but we cannot restore it. The river's reclamation continues to require the energy of local communities, funding from the government and the cooperation of local businesses. It will require political power, civic engagement and money.

NEW BENCHMARKS: GOOD NEWS, BAD NEWS, DIFFICULT NEWS

The good news is that neighborhoods around the river have improved and continue to improve. In the twelve years that I have worked in the West Farms neighborhood, I have seen empty, trash-strewn lots transformed into three- and four-apartment, affordable row houses. The new low-income housing units are often owned and have one apartment occupied by one resident who rents out the other apartments, thus providing much needed funds to pay the mortgage. Additional good news is that frequent testing of the quality of Bronx River water along its entire length is taking place. As a result, observers and concerned citizens will not have to wait long to obtain new benchmarks describing the environmental state of the Bronx River.

The bad news is that fecal coliform (an indicator of the existence of human excrement) remains abundant in the river, especially after it rains. Evaluation of the Bronx River's condition is contained in three summary reports, one published in 2006 by the Bronx River Alliance, one in 2007 for Westchester County Department of Planning and an intermunicipal plan in 2011.[144] Each of these reports indicates high levels of fecal coliform at various "hot spots" in the Bronx River. A detailed statement of coliform pollution of the Bronx River appears in an appendix to the 2006 Ecological Restoration and Management Plan. It reports that seventeen Yonkers storm water overflows continue discharging sewage into the river: "Needless to say, the problem of fecal coliform contamination is an ongoing problem in the Bronx River. These discharges present human health hazards, harm the biological diversity and ecological stability of the Bronx River and impair its ability to support fish propagation."[145] In

New York City's Department of Environmental Protection Combined Sewer Outflow HP 007, just south of East Tremont Avenue and north of 174th Street, continues to supply the river with excrement during a rain storm. *Photo by Bronx River Alliance.*

addition to the Westchester discharges that have been identified as illegal hookups of sanitary sewer pipes to storm water pipes, combined sewer overflows in the Bronx contribute sewage waste to the river's estuary.

The difficult news is that river cleanup is complex. As the history of the Bronx River demonstrates, a river can degrade a certain volume of waste if the amount is not overwhelming. This wonderful capacity meant that indigenous people, the early Europeans and even folks in rural areas well into the nineteenth century did not have to worry much about waste disposal. Nature, with the ability to degrade organic materials, took care of it for them. Today, with runoff from parking lots, roads, golf courses, lawns and the other sources, as well as effluent from the "more than 100 discharge pipes"[146] and combined sewer overflows, the river is easily overwhelmed. When it rains, discharge into the river increases so much that it takes considerable time to degrade and wash away into the East River, itself already overwhelmed with waste.

Sewage waste in water bodies like the Bronx River should be prevented from entering the waterway in the first place. Fortunately, in the New

York City area, this issue is being taken seriously by a fifty-three-member partnership organization with the acronym SWIM (Storm Water Infrastructure Matters). With its original focus on the Bronx River as a pilot area and now a citywide organization, SWIM's goal is to ensure "swimmable waters around New York City through natural, sustainable storm water management practices in our neighborhoods."[147] Today's combined storm water and sewer system was developed in the nineteenth century. Then pipes draining wastewater combined with pipes draining storm water were the generally approved and admired "sanitary" state of the art. Spending money to create a parallel system that keeps sewage separate from storm water will be difficult and expensive but must be implemented.

Just as diners once enjoyed the river, so today increasing numbers of recreational users again enjoy the river experience. Unfortunately, the reports show that sewage still flows into the river. A worthy goal is to have zero discharge into the river. That being said, however, nonpoint-source pollution (runoff from impervious surfaces throughout the watershed are a prime cause of this type of pollution) remains a problem. While the river can handle modest organic waste, minimizing those toxins and eliminating point-source pollution are the next steps toward reclaiming the Bronx River. Eliminating or controlling sources of pollution in a watershed lead not only to a cleaner river and a healthier watershed, it will contribute toward a more vibrant, healthy community overall.[148]

Reclaiming the Bronx River cannot happen without the participation of government, corporations and other businesses, nongovernment organizations, local community groups and numerous individuals. In a complex society, the difficult news is that all these entities, with their competing functions and interests, often work at cross purposes. As the river is cleaned up and as property values increase, landowners and residents may find themselves in conflict with each other. Most of the funding for environmental cleanup comes from business and government. Those organizations and institutions have disproportionate power, while community-based organizations primarily advise or cajole. While participation in decision making by local community groups and individuals will not change the existing power structure, decision makers must seek out and continue being influenced by individuals and local groups, while individuals and local groups must work to affect decisions that are made. As this study demonstrates, individuals working for the cleanup of the Bronx River have influenced its reclamation.

The future is full of challenges for community organizations like the Bronx River Alliance. Maintaining the momentum of broad-based participation in the use and maintenance of the Bronx River Watershed after the initial gains presented here will require adapting to changing residential demographics and the changing composition of the individuals likely to participate in river and community cleanup:

> *Community revitalization is so important. Today kids take existing parks for granted. They weren't there for the struggle to get parks so they can't say "we won this." Today we have users of the parks* [young people] *who didn't have anything to do with this history. We want them to help write the next chapter and see the river as a resource. We struggled to get as far as we have. We must work to incorporate new residents who might otherwise take their amenities for granted into an ongoing process.*[149]

Cultivating civic engagement among new community members requires a special focus on grass-roots organizing. It requires a specific focus, but with the other river cleanup work at hand and with limited funds, this is a task that is often deferred until a later time. The question becomes "How do we involve this new generation of community members and the community at large into the further work of reclamation and the continuing work of maintaining the river as a resource for all to enjoy?"[150] As young people mature, some will become aware of the importance of quality of life as an issue community members can affect. The Bronx River Alliance and other community-based organizations can serve the developing awareness of new generations with leadership, information sharing and funding. As new community members become engaged, they will gain the skills to develop policy initiatives and participate in the decision making that affects their lives.

Changing incomes have and will change another aspect of the demographic composition of community residents. While the number of local activists may be increasing, "there are simply not enough interested local people available to create an active civic infrastructure"[151] in the Bronx because the borough's residents, preoccupied with obtaining their subsistence, have time for little else. As the income of Bronx residents improves, they may become more willing and able to participate in grass-roots environmental work. It would be nice if decision making came from the affected communities even in face of government and business control and funding, but, at least, community preferences and needs must be included in that process. The task of activists is to establish a climate that is receptive to new participants, no matter their income levels.

For the Bronx organizations, maintaining their grass-roots organizing and financial "transparency" will be essential in fostering community involvement in Bronx River reclamation. If successful and sustainable, these excursions in economic democracy could become models for our society. However, the success of such efforts is fragile in an economy driven by private property interests and the pursuit of profit.

EFFORTS TO RECLAIM THE BRONX RIVER AND ITS WATERSHED

A degraded river cannot be improved without also paying attention to the watershed through which it flows. Authors of Bronx River Restoration's *Master Plan* focused on both the river and its watershed as early as 1980. In 2004, Alexie Torres-Fleming, then the executive director of YMPJ, expressed the importance of the relationship between the river and its watershed: "the restoration of a beautiful river…can result in the restoration of whole communities as well."[152] By 2011, the authors of the Intermunicipal Plan, a coalition of Bronx and Westchester organizations, expressed a comprehensive vision of the Bronx River and its watershed as

> *an ecologically healthy river system that is protected by water-sensitive practices and policies in the watershed, supports diverse native aquatic and riparian communities, and helps support economic strength, public health, recreation, and a high quality of life for the communities in the Bronx River and Long Island Sound watersheds.*[153]

The Bronx River has become a model of river cleanup by showing that healthy communities result in a clean watershed and therefore a clean river and vice versa.

When the river was strewn with obstacles, community members had something physical to push against. Now that the river is visibly cleaner, the target for community cohesiveness may not be so easy to find. The Bronx River Alliance's mission of being "in harmonious partnership to protect, improve and restore the Bronx River corridor and greenway" only offers general guidance to river advocates. The Bronx River Alliance's promotion of economic democracy remains one of their greatest triumphs. Required is a nurturing of community members' participation in decision making through as much of a participatory structure of its teams as a maturing organization can maintain, including their inclusion on the board of directors. The structure of that form of civic engagement remains in dynamic flux.

There are a few likely choices for specific next steps in reclaiming the Bronx River as a natural resource and a regional treasure. Some of these steps have already been articulated by river activists. Most important is job creation. While looking for jobs, residents will have difficulty finding the time for civic involvement. There already is significant green job training and retraining in the South Bronx.[154] The focus here is on infrastructure development and reconstruction. Parks need to be built. Building of a greenway along the Bronx River and New York City's much larger waterfront is in process. Training in the South Bronx is taking place in a changing network of organizations, including Sustainable South Bronx, the Point Community Development Corporation, Rocking the Boat, among others. Green roofs are being installed on schools and businesses that will decrease storm water flows. The Bronx River Alliance's Conservation Crew hires some of the folks trained locally but cannot accommodate them all. New venues for green project workers need to be identified.

On a national scale, much needed infrastructure development and reconstruction in environmental projects, but also in roads, bridges, Internet connectivity in rural areas, among other projects, should constitute the next important round of job creation. The nation's infrastructure is in sufficiently poor shape that this expenditure is warranted from an environmental and an economic perspective. This will take national will and funding that in the present political and economic climate does not seem likely. Such national focus should favorably affect the Bronx River

Watershed. Clearly, the Bronx River's reclamation sets an example for infrastructure reconstruction elsewhere.

A second action, necessary for the reclamation of the Bronx River and for its watershed communities, is improved storm water management. The need for storm water management exists not only in the Bronx River's watershed but also in New York City as a whole, in Westchester County and nationally. Water, especially drinkable water, promises to be an increasingly important issue everywhere. Managing storm water appropriately will reduce the pressure on the drinking water supply. It will also reduce the environmental load on nearby water bodies, including the still besieged Bronx River.

THE BRONX RIVER

The Bronx River has played many rolls. First it was a drinking water source, a food source and a means of transportation. Later it was a boundary and a border, a source of power for dams and a location for the disposal of wastes. Then it became a place of recreation and a focus for organizing adjoining communities. From about 1850 on, the river's water quality was degraded by overuse, increased sewage, illegal disposal of pollutants and disregard for the environment. As New York City's only freshwater river, the Bronx River is an environmental gem that remains the focus of various groups trying to clean it up.

While river advocates discuss "restoring" the river, the river cannot be restored to what it was before 1700. It has been straightened. It has been, and continues to be, used as a sewer. It has been used as a dumping place. And the population around it has expanded by several orders of magnitude. But it can, once again, be beautified. It can be cleaned up to a point. It might again become swimmable. It might become fishable. It already is used for recreation. It is unlikely, at least any time soon, to become a source of drinking water, with the important exception that its former headwaters consist of a thirty-two-billion-gallon reservoir that is part of New York City's drinking water supply system (a benefit to the city that caused a significant diversion of water, lowering downstream water quality).

Bronx River Alliance executive director Linda Cox (in the stern of the lead canoe) escorts paddlers down the Bronx River channel. *Photo by Bronx River Alliance.*

That the river was once a hidden feature of the inner city is undeniable. But the Bronx River is no longer hidden. Accidental spills into the river now result in quick cleanup activities by appropriate agencies. The handling of the Con Edison spill caused by the Dunwoodie Substation fire on November 4, 2009, is revealing. Shortly after that mishap, Con Edison and its New York State regulator, the Department of Environmental Conservation (DEC), came together around a conference table at the Bronx River Alliance headquarters[155] to explain that an electrical short ignited the insulating oil. According to Con Edison and DEC, while the containment area was large enough to capture the oil, it was the additional volume of fire-suppressing foam that led to an overflow into the river. Con Edison expected it would take about a month of work and observation before the river would be restored to its prespill conditions. The cleanup and the promises of future safety precautions by the state and the corporation were less remarkable than the contribution of the Bronx River Alliance staff. They were not the first people on the scene nor were they included in the early rounds of notifications, but they proved to be the most knowledgeable about the Bronx River's unique flows. Producing skilled, knowledgeable individuals working on the river remains an important focus of the Bronx River Alliance:

> *The Bronx River Alliance is working to create a climate of organizations and individuals who are smart and knowledgeable about water management. It is fostering a network of groups and individuals with knowledge and skills. The South Bronx has become a hope of environmentalism and environmental networks but it is not yet widely recognized as that.*[156]

The alliance continues its work to incorporate the decision making of community members. To the extent that it continues such patterns of democratization, it needs to be closely watched and emulated.

With the Bronx River's beautification, property values around it will likely increase, placing pressure on existing residents to leave while more affluent populations move in. Such pressures must be resisted by assuring the continued availability of truly affordable housing. The river must remain accessible to members of all classes. Cleaning up the Bronx River is but one step in a much larger project of reclaiming the many natural resources that have been damaged by industry, an inattentive government and recklessly greedy individuals. As such, Bronx River beautification stands as a national monument to urban environmental riparian reclamation. It is an example of a movement aimed at democratizing society and at reclaiming lost natural treasures.

Epilogue

At 9:00 a.m. on a Saturday morning, more than fifty people were already milling around Olinville Park at 219th Street in the larger Shoelace Park. Tables had been set up. Almost ninety red and green canoes were neatly lined up on the grass. Release forms needed to be signed. The assembled crowd networked with each other. They listened to the safety talk, put on new T-shirts and carried their assigned canoes to the launch site. Members of the Conservation Crew in waders, stood poised, waist deep in the river's channel to help participants into their canoes.[157] On this bright sunny day, paddlers glided down the Shoelace channel, most of them sufficiently experienced to navigate the Bronx River.

Canoeists portaged around the three dams, each time with the cheery assistance of the crew. On the water and under the canopy of trees shading it, they could hear the urban sounds of the Bronx, but mostly they did not see cars, trucks or elevated trains. They could have been on a small river anywhere. Paddlers passed under bridges, went through the New York Botanical Garden and the Bronx Zoo. Most of them avoided the rocks of the faster water of the Bronx River Rapids near the warehouse that houses the Bronx River Art Center. They passed other notable sites, including Drew Gardens, the 174th Street Bridge, Starlight Park, Fannie Lou Hamer Freedom High School and the Westchester Avenue Bridge, over which the "6" train roars. Their destination was the then incomplete

Above: Canoes and canoeists waiting to participate in the Amazing Bronx River Flotilla at 219th Street Park. *Photo by Bronx River Alliance.*

Left: A Conservation Crew member lends a helping hand portaging around the 181st Street Dam, the former DeLancy/Lydig mill dam. *Photo by Bronx River Alliance.*

Just after the announcement of significant funding for river cleanup and that 1999 would be the year of the Bronx River, politicians and activists celebrated at Starlight Park. From left: Congressman José E. Şerrano, then assemblyman (now borough president) Ruben Diaz Jr., founder of Sustainable South Bronx Majora Carter, then New York State governor George Pataki, then New York City park commissioner Henry J. Stern, founder and former executive director of Youth Ministries for Peace and Justice Alexie Torres-Fleming and Bronx River Working Group executive director Jenny Hoffner. *Photo by Youth Ministries for Peace and Justice.*

The Bronx River passes under an approach to the Bronx River Parkway in Tuckahoe, NY. *Photo by Maarten de Kadt.*

Concrete Plant Park, where the waterborne participants joined a land-based community festival celebrating the Bronx River.

The Bronx River has become a place of celebration, community activism, and a genuine amenity to the communities that occupy its watershed. In turn, New York City's only freshwater river is generously reclaiming and renewing each of us in the process. Hopefully, the inspiring story of the Bronx River's comeback will spur continued renewal of this river and of rivers like it. Reclaiming and enjoying this twenty-three-mile river is only a small part of reclaiming natural resources everywhere.

Acknowledgements

I am extremely greatful to my students and colleagues at Fannie Lou Hamer Freedom High School for introducing me to the Bronx River. There, Lloyd Ultan, the Bronx historian, presented his view of Bronx and Bronx River history to teachers at a professional development seminar.[158] In addition, he has been a willing respondent to my questions about the Bronx and the river for which it is named. Frank Pandolfo and I cotaught the River Class at Fannie Lou Hamer Freedom High School. Frank taught the science, and I taught the social studies, though each of us did a bit of each. Early in this project, Frank and I took an excursion to learn about the upper reaches of the Bronx River. That trip produced some of the images used in this book. Finally, in the late editing stage of this project, Frank helped answer a question that arose concerning the location of the Horton Tannery in White Plains near to where Frank lives by embarking on several last-minute excursions to verify this mill's location.

Staff of the Bronx River Alliance—Anne-Marie Runfola, Maggie Scott Greenfield, Michelle Williams and Stephen DeVillo—have provided information, shared ideas, offered encouragement and given feedback on earlier drafts of this work. A number of librarians and archivists have helped me find information for this project: Westchester County Archives and Historical Society, Bronx Historical Society, New York Historical Society, the Library of the New York Botanical Garden, Dan Donovan of the Bronx Borough President's Map Office, Ken Cob of the New York City Municipal Archive and former mayor Philip A. White of the Tuckahoe Historical Society and his helpful staff.

A number of people have been generous with their time by permitting me to interview them: David DeLucia, director of Park Facilities, Westchester County; David Shuffler, Youth Ministries for Peace and Justice; Hank Stroosbants; Linda Cox, Bronx River Alliance; Louie DiNapoli, owner of the Old Stone Mill and Restaurant; Majora Carter, the Majora Carter Group; and Mike Carew. Each of these folks, in different ways, has a continuing interest in the well-being of Bronx River Valley communities and of the river itself. Without their hard work, the reclaiming of the Bronx River would not be as far along as it is. Jack Raskin, Joyce Miller and Nat Yalowitz were eager to describe to me their childhood remembrances of the Bronx River.

A number of folks have read various drafts of this work: Chuck Boothby, Michael Black, Theodore Steinberg and my children, Jesse Campoamor and Sonja de Kadt. I particularly want to single out Dart Westphal, whose careful early reading, insightful comments, deep knowledge of Bronx history and constant encouragement has greatly enriched this work. Betty Mackintosh, Damian Griffin, Linda Cox and Resa Dimino read the penultimate draft of this work. Each of these readers pointed out errors of fact or tone. I accepted most of their suggestions and at my peril rejected some of them. Their combined knowledge of the environment, planning, the Bronx River and clear writing helped transform this work into its final form.

Matthew Croswell researched and designed the four maps in this book that help the reader answer the question, "Where is that?"

The History Press team transformed my manuscript into a book. Whitney Tarella guided me through the complex process of arriving at an agreement to publish this book and offered encouragement on images, on tables and on maps and offered comments on the penultimate draft. Through her knowledge of style and careful editing, Amber Allen improved the final draft still further.

Karen Smith—my wife, my friend and my partner—has edited and commented on *every* draft of this work. This project wouldn't be half what it is if I didn't have her insight, intelligence, wit, excitement, pride and respect for the project; questioning; and love. She has enriched this work, but more importantly, she enriches my life.

While I am a ten-year member of the board of the Bronx River Alliance and, in 2011, became vice chair, and while I have asked for and taken comments from people either on the board or on the staff of the Bronx River Alliance, the material in this book has not been authorized or approved by the Bronx River Alliance. And in spite of the good advice I have received from those listed above, I have gathered the information, interpreted the materials and am responsible for the content of this book.

Appendix
Timeline

pre-1639	Indigenous peoples use the river for food, water and transportation.
1639	Jonas Bronck begins farming near what is now the Bronx River.
1643	Jonas Bronck dies.
1664	British take over New York.
1664	West Farms settled by English farmers.
1680	Richardson Mill Dam is built (approximate date). Later owned by the DeLancy and then the Lydig families.
1776	George Washington escapes from Brooklyn through Westchester and the Bronx River Valley.
1792	Lorillard Tobacco Company moves to a mill on the Bronx River.
1799	William Weston's report of Bronx River water quality.
1805	A cotton mill begins operation in Tuckahoe, New York.
1809	The Bronx River Paint Company is incorporated.
1814	A stone mill house is constructed in Tuckahoe, New York.
1840	The Lorillard Tobacco Company replaces its wooden mills with a stone building.
1841	The New York and Harlem Railroad reaches Fordham.
1844	The New York and Harlem Railroad reaches White Plains.
1870	The Lorillard Snuff Mill ceases operation when the tobacco company moves elsewhere.

1873	New York, New Haven & Hartford Railroad begins to operate along the Bronx River.
1874	The territory west of the Bronx River becomes part of New York City forming the 23rd and 24th Wards.
1881	A manufactured gas plant is operating on the Bronx River in West Farms.
1885	The first Kensico Dam is completed.
1888	Lydig Mill ceases operation.
1888	Bronx Park is formed.
1888	The Lorillard Snuff Mill becomes part of Bronx Park.
1895	The territory east of the Bronx River becomes part of New York City.
1896	The Bronx Valley Sewer Commission declares the Bronx River to be an "open sewer."
1907	Bronx Parkway Commission is established.
1911	Sewer built next to the northern part of the Bronx River.
1913	By this time, the Stone Mill is using steam power.
1915	The present Kensico Dam is completed.
1925	Bronx River Parkway completed.
1928	Burroughs-Wellcome Pharmaceuticals buys the Stone Mill property in Tuckahoe.
1952	The Hunts Point Water Treatment Plant opens.
1952	Bronx River Parkway extension completed.
1974	Bronx River Restoration formed.
1980	Bronx River Restoration *Master Plan* issued.
1987	Transit Mix Concrete fails, leaving a vacant property.
1989	The *Bronx Queen* runs aground and sinks.
1992	The Old Stone Mill in Tuckahoe receives landmark status.
1999	First Golden Ball celebration.
1999	First Amazing Bronx River Flotilla.
2001	Memorandum of Agreement between Bronx Zoo and New York State attorney general.
2001	Bronx River Alliance formed.
2002	Heavy concrete blocks are placed along the Bronx River to prevent further dumping.
2006	Ecological Restoration and Management Plan published.

2007	Bronx River Watershed Assessment and Management Plan published.
2007	Hunts Point Riverside Park opens.
2009	Transformer fire in Yonkers sends insulating oil to the Bronx River.
2009	Concrete Plant Park opens.
2011	Bronx River Intermunicipal Watershed Management Plan published.
2011	West Farms Rapids Park opens.
2012	Completion of Starlight Park scheduled.

Glossary

The following is a short list of terms used here to describe aspects of the Bronx River. Most of these definitions come from the U.S. Environmental Protection Agency and the National Oceanographic and Atmospheric Administration. If the reader is interested in further information, these agencies are a good place to start.

Anadromous fish: born in fresh water, it spends most of its life in the sea and returns to fresh water to spawn. Alewives are an anadromous fish recently introduced into the Bronx River.

Balancing reservoir: also called a terminal reservoir or a distribution reservoir, as it forms part of the final stages of the water collection system before water enters into the distribution system. It balances the demand for water in the distribution system with the flow of water from collecting reservoirs. The Kensico Reservoir is a balancing reservoir.

Bioaccumulation: general term describing a process by which chemicals are taken up by an organism either directly from exposure to a contaminated medium or by consumption of food containing the chemical.

Estuary: a complex, partially enclosed coastal body of water where fresh water from the land dilutes saltwater from the ocean. Ocean tides cause estuaries to rise and fall, and at the same time, they cause them to ebb and flow but not necessarily in the same rhythm. The Bronx River happens to have a rather simple estuary south of East Tremont Avenue where there the mixing of salt and fresh water is characterized more by layering with the denser salt water on the bottom, while much of the fresh water remains on the surface.

Headwaters: the sources of water that create our rivers, streams and lakes. The original headwaters of the Bronx River are under the Kensico Reservoir.

Point-source and nonpoint-source pollution: point-source pollution is pollution that comes from a well-defined place. Much more common is nonpoint-source pollution that comes from unidentified places.

Seine net: a large hanging net with weights at the bottom and floats at the top.

Watershed: the area of land where all of the water that is under it or drains off of it goes into the same body of water. The Bronx River has a long, narrow watershed, as indicated on the Bronx River map on page 8.

Wetlands: those areas that are inundated or saturated by surface or groundwater at a frequency and duration sufficient to support, and that under normal circumstances do support, a prevalence of vegetation typically adapted for life in saturated soil conditions. Wetlands generally include swamps, marshes, bogs and similar areas. Most Bronx River wetlands have been filled in.

Notes

Preface

1. For example: Reuters, "Fire damages Con Ed Transformer in Dunwoodie, NY," November 4, 2009; Shelley Ng, "Fire Tears Through Con Ed Substation," PIX 11, November 4, 2009; and Associated Press, "Con Ed Fined $700,000 for Yonkers Substation Fire," July 28, 2010. Four months before the accident, a consultant to the utility identified the improperly functioning system at the substation that caused the fire. As a result of this event, Con Edison eventually received a $700,000 fine from the New York State Department of Environmental Conservation.
2. For a convenient topographical reference, see: Trails.com, http://www.trails.com/topo.aspx?state=NY (accessed December 1, 2010). This site returns a location's elevation above sea level.
3. Both the Hudson and the Hutchinson Rivers are estuaries by the time they reach New York City, and the Harlem and East Rivers are not rivers at all—they are tidal straits.
4. Caro, *The Power Broker*.
5. This and other technical language used to describe rivers is defined in the Glossary.
6. See de Kadt, "The Bronx River" for an exploration of this experience.
7. Another way to construct this phrase would be to say "the human and the natural environment" or "human and natural," but these place

humans against the environment. As I see it, humans are part of the environment.

1. PRODUCTION FOR USE: MINIMAL IMPACT

8. Mann, *1491*; Cronon, *Changes in the Land*; and Merchant, *Ecological Revolutions*.
9. Merchant, *Ecological Revolutions*, 76, 80.
10. Ibid., 84.
11. Jenkins, *The Story of the Bronx*, 25. Today the name Lenape is used to include a larger confederation of pre-Columbian peoples, including some of those mentioned here, stretching from Delaware to the lower Hudson Valley.
12. Bolton, *Indian Life*, 137–38; Cantwell and diZerega Wall, *Unearthing Gotham*, 114; Greenburgh Nature Center, *Bronx River Retrospective*, 6; and Ultan, "History of the Bronx River."
13. Cumbler, *Reasonable Use*, 15.
14. Merchant, *Ecological Revolutions*, 75. Cantwell and diZerega Wall, *Unearthing Gotham*, 114, place more emphasis on seafood as part of indigenous people's diet:

    > *The evidence we have…suggests that although there may have been small gardens, agricultural foods were not a major part of the diet during the Late Woodland in coastal New York. But as is always the case, we need properly dug and analyzed sites, preferably ones with well-preserved plant and animal remains, to advance the argument.*

    So comparison to indigenous peoples in other parts of the territory north and east of New York needs to be accepted cautiously.
15. Bolton Jr., *History of the County of Westchester*, v. 2, 145.
16. Cantwell and diZerega Wall, *Unearthing Gotham*.
17. Cronon, *Changes in the Land*; Merchant, *Ecological Revolutions*, specifically page 74; and Sanderson, *Mannahatta*, 128.
18. Merchant, in *Ecological Revolutions*, has an extended discussion of the complexities of the physical and social production and reproduction

(see in particular Chapter 1: "Ecology and History") that she applies to New England Indians prior to the arrival of the Europeans. Their form of production and reproduction dramatically changed with the arrival of the Europeans. The revolution of ecology (Merchant's concept) in the Aquehung Valley was likely similar.

19. Mann, *1491*; Diamond, *Collapse.*
20. Cronon, *Changes in the Land*, 42. I'm using New England, a much larger territory than Aquehung's watershed, comparatively as an indicator to what population in the watershed may have been.
21. Merchant, *Ecological Revolutions*, 39.
22. Sanderson, *Mannahatta*, 112. Sanderson is using Mannahatta and Manhattan to refer to the island today known as Manhattan.
23. MacDonald, "The Bronx River"; Greenburgh Nature Center, *Bronx River Retrospective*, 6, uses the same number.

2. PRODUCING A SURPLUS FOR TRADE

24. Merchant, *Ecological Revolutions*, 91.
25. Burrows and Wallace, *Gotham*, 9.
26. Cronon, *Changes in the Land*, 75.
27. Jenkins, *The Story of the Bronx*, 26.
28. Burrows and Wallace, *Gotham*, 37.
29. Morrisanina is mentioned in Burrows and Wallace, *Gotham*, 36.
30. Randall Comfort, quoted in Rachlin, *History of the Bronx Borough.* This speculation likely relies on that of Robert Bolton Jr. (Jenkins does not seem to think the land went that far north), who in 1848 wrote the following indefinite statement about the 182nd Street location: "Here it is probable that Jonas Bronck (from whom the river derives its name) erected a mill and laid out a plantation as early as 1639." Bolton Jr., *History of the County of Westchester*, 426.
31. Jenkins, *The Story of the Bronx*, 28. Jenkins used Bronck's Last Will and Testament as a source for the listing of the artifacts passed along to his heirs.
32. I have seen various spellings of Bronck's name. As a rule, I use "Bronck," the spelling favored by Ultan, *The Northern Borough.*

33. The Bronck Museum, Coxsackie, near Albany, New York, August 9, 2009.
34. Ultan, *The Northern Borough*, 8–12, revised from Ultan, "Jonas Bronck," 53–67. Greenburgh Nature Center, *Bronx River Retrospective*, 9.
35. Ultan, *The Northern Borough*, 11.
36. Burrows and Wallace, *Gotham*; Ultan, "History of the Bronx River"; Rachlin, *History of the Bronx Borough*; Ultan and Hermalyn, *The Birth of the Bronx*, 4, also discuss Bronck.
37. Steinberg, *Nature Incorporated*.
38. Cumbler, *Reasonable Use*.
39. See the Woonasquatucket River Watershed Council, http://www.woonasquatucket.org/index.htm (accessed December 7, 2010). Thanks to Jenny Hoffner for alerting me to this historical river gem.
40. Jenkins, *The Story of the Bronx*, 105, 217, 294; and New York City Department of Parks, "Van Cortlandt Park," http://www.nycgovparks.org/sub_your_park/vt_van_cortlandt_park/vt_van_cort_12.html and "Van Cortlandt Park: Tibbetts Brook," http://www.nycgovparks.org/sub_your_park/historical_signs/hs_historical_sign.php?id=8183 (accessed December 9, 2009). Tidal mills existed near Hogg's Island and on the Harlem River. The city acquired title to property that would become Van Cortlandt Park on December 12, 1888, as part of a major purchase of parkland including Bronx Park. Tibbetts Brook is the current name of Tippetts Brook, transformed from the original name of George Tippett.
41. Ultan, *The Northern Borough*, 21, 46.
42. Cronon, *Changes in the Land*, 75.
43. Jenkins, *The Story of the Bronx*, 44.
44. Bolton Jr., *History of the County of Westchester*, vol. 2, 426.
45. Jenkins, *The Story of the Bronx*, 151, 167.
46. Weston, "On the Practicability."
47. Galusha, *Liquid Assets*, 15.

3. Industrial Production Develops

48. Greenburgh Nature Center, *Bronx River Retrospective*, inside cover and 10, indicate there were twelve mills on the Bronx River, but the

author's attempt to confirm that exact number has been problematic. See the footnote 63 in "Other Milldams" section.

49. See Glossary.
50. Dunlap, "From Tobacco Leaves."
51. National Historic Landmarks Program, "Lorillard Snuff Mill," http://tps.cr.nps.gov/nhl/detail.cfm?ResourceId=1727&ResourceType=Building (accessed January 21, 2011).
52. In addition to Dunlap, this Lorillard Snuff Mill history relies on a document dated November 15, 2001, found at the Botanical Garden's Library and in Ultan, *The Northern Borough*, 125–26.
53. Ishiguri, "Secrets Behind the Stone." Samuel Slater built his Pawtucket, Rhode Island cotton mill in 1793.
54. Ibid., 9.
55. George Barker Hodgman, biography, *The National Cyclopaedia of American Biography*, http://books.google.com/books?id=i-cDAAAAYAAJ&pg=PA324&lpg=PA324&dq=rubber+manufacturing+process+hodgman&source=bl&ots=jD1dQC9SbD&sig=NhpGWpv5B1s7tDBcuv7CO5QBNvY&hl=en&ei=DeK5TMuRJYWKlwfFkZy5DQ&sa=X&oi=book_result&ct=result&resnum=1&sqi=2&ved=0CB4Q6AEwAA#v=onepage&q=rubber%20manufacturing%20process%20hodgman&f=false (accessed October 16, 2010).
56. Unlabeled photograph of the Old Stone Mill site. circa 1913, Tuckahoe Historical Society, October 6, 2010.
57. *Revised Statutes of the State of New York* (Albany, 1829), 559, http://books.google.com/books?id=KJEDAAAAQAAJ&pg=PA559&dq=Bronx+rIVER+pAINT+cOMPANY&cd=1#v=onepage&q=Bronx%20rIVER%20pAINT%20cOMPANY&f=false (accessed January 12, 2010).
58. See Glossary.
59. *Laws of the State of New York*, Chapter 118 (CXVIII), "An Act to Improve the Navigation of the River Bronx," http://books.google.com/books?pg=PA130&lpg=PA130&dq=%22bronx%20river%20paint%20company%22&sig=AdEamcwpLfdl-HEUaohVwa9jv-g&ei=nhhJS8GDO8-JlAex3_gN&ct=result&id=n1Y4AAAAIAAJ&ots=UWyEXJFqjC&output=text (accessed January 12, 2010).

60. Damian Griffin and Stephen DeVillo of the Bronx River Alliance drew this story to my attention on January 9, 2010.
61. Bolton, Obituary. New York City established Bronx Park through the use of eminent domain in 1888 after a commission established in 1881 determined the value of the forty properties taken to form the park. The estate of Ann Bolton was one of the recipients of payment for property taken. The *New York Times* paid frequent attention to the taking of property for Bronx Park: *New York Times*, November 27, 1888; October 6, 1888; June 27, 1888; October 6, 1888; December 28, 1888; February 13, 1889. Also see Gonzalez, *The Bronx*.
62. *New York State Reporter*, vol. 70 (N.p.: October 18, 1895), 199.
63. Ultan, *The Northern Borough*, 142, 185, 195 and 247; Hermalyn, "History of the Bronx River," 8.
64. *New York Supplement*, vol. 35, (N.p.: 1889), 578.
65. Macdonald, "The Bronx River," tells us there were eight beaver dams in what is now Westchester and more in the Bronx, "all later made into mills by the settlers." As of the date of publication of this book, the exact locations of the twelve mills have not been identified. The map at the beginning of this chapter indicates the known mill locations. It is uncertain as to whether there were two or three mills covered by the Kensico Reservoir and whether there was a mill north of the Scarsdale Train Station in the Mill Stream Diversion, though that diversion is likely to have been the water-power source for the gunpowder mill. Bronx River Paint Company's location is also unknown but might have been in what is now the Bronx Zoo. The White Plains tannery could have been in any of several locations but is most likely to have been close to boundaries of Harrison, North Castle and White Plains on a Bronx River tributary coming from Silver Lake. Silver Lake used to be called Horton's Pond. David DeLucia, personal interview, April 5, 2011; Frank Pandolfo, personal interview April 8, 2011, and May 2, 2011. Pandolfo reports the existence of a mill site in the northern location and gets some of his information from Renoda Hoffman, *It Happened in Old White Plains*, n.p.: self-published, 1989.
66. The Wrights' mills are discussed in North Castle Historical Society, *North Castle History*, vol. 32 (New Rochelle, NY: D&M Press, Inc., 2005).

67. New York State Department of Health, in conjunction with Con Edison, "Fact Sheet: Starlight Park Site," February 2003, says the plant was built prior to 1893. See also GEI Consultants, "East 173rd Street Works (Starlight Park) Operable Unit No. 1 (OU-1)," August 24, 2004, http://www.gothamgas.com/StarlightPark/Documents/E173%20Final%20RAWP-txt-tbl-fig-app%208-20-04.pdf (accessed January 14, 2010). I use the 1881 date based on *New York Times*, "Filthy State of the Bronx River," December 7, 1881. The site is depicted on Insurance Maps of the City of New York.
68. Louis A Risse, "Public Works," in *The Great North Side or Borough of the Bronx*, North Side Board of Trade (New York: 1897), 179.
69. *New York Times*, "Filthy State of the Bronx River," December 7, 1881.

4. A Place to Live

70. *Report of the Bronx Parkway Commission*, 53; Gonzalez, *The Bronx*, 11.
71. Christopher Gray, "Where Ghost Passengers Await Very Late Trains," *New York Times*, November 25, 2009; Wikipedia, "Harlem River and Port Chester Railroad, November 14, 2009," http://en.wikipedia.org/wiki/Harlem_River_and_Port_Chester_Railroad,_November_14,_2009 (accessed January 6, 2010); Earl Pleasants.com, http://www.earlpleasants.com/search_1.asp (accessed January 6, 2010), search on Harlem River; Jackson, *Crabgrass Frontier*.
72. Jackson, *Crabgrass Frontier*, p. 70; Gonzalez, *The Bronx*, 22; and Ultan, *The Northern Borough*, 142.
73. See, for example, *New York Times*, "Filthy State of the Bronx River," December 7, 1881, and Department of Public Parks: Adopted Map "D" No 45, 1884, at the Bronx Borough President's map room. Chuck Boothby, whose Maine home features two privies, reminded me "that in the spirit of sustainability, we, as a culture, are exploring what it would mean to return to privies in the updated form of composting toilets." Boothby, personal communication, February 2011.
74. Robert Jackson says, "The most important municipal boundary adjustment in American history occurred in 1898, when Andrew

Haswell Green's lifelong dream of a Greater New York City was realized." Jackson, *Crabgrass Frontier*, 142.

75. Gray Williams, "Westchester County: Historic Suburban Neighborhoods," in *Westchester: The American Suburb*, edited by Roger Panetta (Hudson River Museum, 2006), 184.
76. Galusha, *Liquid Assets*, 53.
77. New York City Department of Environmental Protection, "Bronx River Waterbody/Watershed Facility Plan Report," chapter 2, 1. This quotation contains this book's first use of the word "reach" in a riparian (river-related) sense. Here the word means the stretch of water visible between bends in a river or channel, according to Free Dictionary.com, http://www.thefreedictionary.com/reach (accessed January 22, 2011).
78. Galusha, *Liquid Assets*, appendix, and New York City Department of Environmental Protection, http://www.nyc.gov/html/dep/html/watershed_protection/kensico.shtml (accessed April 28, 2011). Also see Glossary.
79. See the quotation from Weston, "On the Practicability," in Chapter 3, 27–28.
80. *Report of the Bronx Valley Sewer Commission*, 4, emphasis as in the original.
81. Jenkins, *The Story of the Bronx*, 33.
82. Miller, *Fat of the Land*, 42.
83. *Report of the Bronx Parkway Commission*, 14. In 1910, the Metropolitan Sewerage Commission of New York reported, "The Passaic River, the Rahway River, the Bronx River, Gowanus and Newton Creeks, and the Harlem River have become little else than open sewers." *New York Times*, "Calls Nearby Rivers Mere Open Sewers," March 7, 1910.

5. Reclaiming the River

84. In 2001 the New York State attorney general's office signed a memorandum in which the zoo agreed to stop discharging untreated sewage from animal grazing areas into the Bronx River and to build a $1 million river walkway now open to the public.
85. F. Hopkinson Smith, "A Day at Laguerre's," in *A Day at Laguerre's and Other Days* (New York: Houghton Mifflin, 1892), 10. But also see *New*

York Times, "Ou L'on Parle Anglais," February 23, 1901, which places this particular bucolic vision, though not the general idea, in doubt: "One difficulty with ["A Day at Laguerre's"]...seems to be that there was no original to that charming piece of fancy work, which was, so far as our memory serves, a composite picture freely and deftly touched with the author's inimitable 'chique.'" Thank you, Damian Griffin, for drawing this comment to my attention.

86. Guy Griffin and James Brown, "Westchester County Solves Some Sewerage Problems," *Sewage and Industrial Wastes* 28, no. 1 (January 1956), 18–27.
87. New York City Department of Environmental Protection, "Secrets of New York: The Sewers," http://www.nyc.gov/html/dep/html/environmental_education/secrets_of_new_york_vod01.shtml (accessed January 27, 2010); Elizabeth Barlow, "New York: A Once and Future Arcadia," *New York* (November 29, 1971); Goldman, *Building New York's Sewers*. Except as noted, this and the previous paragraph is a summary of Goldman's work.
88. Offices of the Commissioner of Street Improvements, Map Showing Sewerage Districts in the 23rd and 24th Wards, December 31, 1892, located in the Bronx Borough President's office.
89. Louis F. Haffen, "Department of Street Improvements," and Louis A Risse, "Public Works," in *The Great North Side or Borough of the Bronx*, 55, 185; Jenkins, *The Story of the Bronx*, 181, 217. While much of Jenkins's work needs to be read with a grain of salt, these reports of sewer construction are in the words of a contemporary of the time that work is being accomplished, putting their accuracy beyond much doubt.
90. New York State Department of Environmental Conservation, *Descriptive Data of Municipal Wastewater Treatment Plants in New York State*, January 2004, A1–A11.
91. *Report of the Bronx Parkway Commission*, 8.
92. Jim Conniff, personal communications with the author and with the Bronx River Alliance, December 2009.
93. *Report of the Bronx Parkway Commission*, 59–61.
94. Ibid., 11, 14. See also page 28 for an additional discussion of sewers constructed by the commission.

95. Outline Map of New York Harbor & Vicinity Showing Main Tidal Flow, Sewer Outlets, Shellfish Beds & Analysis Points Accompanying Report of New York Bay Pollution Commission, 1905, located in New York City Municipal Archives. Thanks to Ken Cob for identifying this map for me.
96. *Report of the Bronx Parkway Commission*, 33.
97. Ibid., 14, 22.
98. Ibid., 8.
99. See NYRoads.com, "Bronx River Parkway," http://www.nycroads.com/roads/bronx-river/ (accessed February 9, 2010). The story of the building of the Bronx River Parkway, both as a parkway and as the first limited-access parkway, is an important story of historical and environmental consequence, but that story is outside of the focus of the environmental history of the Bronx River.
100. Ultan, *The Northern Borough*, 259. While there are three useful histories of the Bronx during this period (Ultan, *The Northern Borough*; Jonnes, *South Bronx Rising*; Gonzalez, *The Bronx*), none of them concentrate on the history of the Bronx River.
101. Jackson, *Crabgrass Frontier*, 197–98.
102. Craig Steven Wilder, personal communication. Professor Wilder collected and shared the HOLC map for the Bronx as well as the HOLC descriptions of the areas mentioned in the text.
103. "History 1920–1983: Westchester Comes of Age," http://www3.westchestergov.com/index.php?option=com_content&view=article&id=2620&Itemid=204496 (accessed May 2, 2011).
104. Wikipedia.org, "Starlight Park," http://en.wikipedia.org/wiki/Starlight_Park (accessed March 12, 2010).
105. Ultan, *The Northern Borough*, 263.
106. Milton Bracker, "Bronx River's Trout Scorn City's 'Incompleat' Anglers: Motley Throngs Match Wits With 560 Fish, Which Come Off Much the Better—They Snub All Lures, Even Curtain Rod," *New York Times*, April 7, 1935.
107. Nat Yalowitz, interview, March 16, 2010.
108. Jack Raskin, interview, April 10, 2010.
109. Joyce Miller, interview, March 15, 2010.

110. For a description of Moses's people-be-damned, autocratic road building methods in the East Tremont section Bronx (not far from the Bronx River), see Caro, *The Power Broker*, Chapter 37, "One Mile."

6. Another Cleanup

111. See for example Ultan, *The Northern Borough*; Gonzalez, *The Bronx*; Jonnes, *South Bronx Rising*; Smith, *Report from Engine Co. 82*; Mahler, *The Bronx Is Burning*.

112. Stewart, "A River Rises," *New York Times*, December 3, 2000. See also Stewart, "In Bronx, A Plan for Reeling in Fish, Not Cars," *New York Times*, November 20, 1999. My students and I attended the news conference held by parks commissioner Henry J. Stern on November 19, 1999, at Starlight Park and reported by Stewart, "In Bronx," 1999, where we saw a rusted car suspended in the air by heavy equipment behind the speakers.

113. Stewart, "A River Rises," *New York Times*, December 3, 2000.

114. Bronx River Restoration, *Master Plan*, 144–46. A photo of the 174th Street combined storm and sanitary sewer appears on page 107 in Chapter 8.

115. Ibid., 12.

116. Grassi, "The Development."

117. In 1997, I came to the Bronx as a new social studies teacher. It would take me two years to discover the existence of the then hidden Bronx River that ran only two hundred yards from the school and to realize that it could be used as a classroom. Bronx River Restoration personnel trained me how to test and teach students how to test the quality of the Bronx River's water. See de Kadt, "The Bronx River."

118. Jenny Hoffner, e-mail to the author, August 20, 2010.

119. The story of the formation and the process of the Bronx River Working Group is well told in Grassi, "The Development."

120. Majora Carter, personal communication, October 25, 2010.

121. Jenny Hoffner, e-mail to the author, August 20, 2010.

122. Grassi tells us there were thirty-five participating organizations by the end of 1998, and that by the end of 2000, sixty-five groups had become involved.

123. My students and I benefitted from the environmental education element of Bronx River Restoration's vision. Part of their mission was to teach teachers the art of water testing. I took their classes and learned how to test for dissolved oxygen and pH. I used my newfound skills to teach my students how to evaluate the Bronx River's water. By so doing, a generation of Fannie Lou Hamer Freedom High School students learned the river existed, its history and an appreciation of environmental issues.

7. The Amazing Bronx River Cleanup

124. Bronx River Alliance, "What We Do," http://bronxriver.org/?pg=content&p=aboutus&m1=1 (accessed March 28, 2010).
125. For an extended discussion of economic democracy as distinct from the elite politics of the political left and right in this country, see Panayotakis, "Capitalism, Socialism, and Economic Democracy."
126. Bronx River Alliance, "Bronx River Conservation Crew," http://bronxriver.org/?pg=content&p=aboutus&m1=1&m2=1&m3=15 (accessed April 5, 2010).
127. Author's interview with Linda Cox, November 18, 2010.
128. To learn about the broad array of Bronx River Alliance activities, go to their website at www.BronxRiver.org, where you will find a wealth of information and also see the several environmental reports referenced later and listed in Table 5.
129. Bruner Foundation, Inc. "2009 Rudy Bruner Award," 70. This is a comprehensive review of the identification of the land, the planning for the park, its construction and its current use.
130. Ibid., 74.
131. For New York City Department of Parks and Recreation's announcement of an award received by this park, see *Daily Plant*, "Hunts Point Riverside Park Wins Rudy Bruner National Award For Urban Excellence," July 8, 2009, http://www.nycgovparks.org/sub_newsroom/daily_plants/daily_plant_main.php?id=21978 (accessed April 5, 2010).
132. The site's pre-1987 occupant, Transit-Mix Concrete, went out of business because its principal owner, Edward J. Halloran, faced

federal and state price-fixing charges and spent some time in jail. Ronald Smothers, "Company in Federal Price-Fixing Closes," *New York Times*, August 16, 1987; Selwyn Raab, "Monopoly Is Seen In Concrete Sales," *New York Times*, June 14, 1984. In regard to the *Bronx Queen*, see Aqua Explorers, Inc./Shipwreck Expo, "The Bronx Queen Shipwreck." Captain Mike Carew, who performed underwater maintenance on the vessel before it sank, told me the *Bronx Queen* was in pretty bad shape even before it went aground. Mike Carew, personal communication February 23, 2011. In addition, Dart Westphal, on numerous occasions, has recounted stories of the *Bronx Queen*. Dart Westphal, personal communications.

133. Diversion of truck traffic from residential streets would be accomplished in other ways, as a result of community scoping meetings that took place during the design of the Hunts Point Riverside Park.
134. David Shuffler, interview with author, December 17, 2010.
135. Adolfo Carrión Jr. was the Bronx Borough president until February 2009. Ruben Diaz Jr. took over in April 2009.
136. It was at the edge of this park that my students and I did our first examination of Bronx River water quality as long ago as 1998.
137. New York State Department of Health, in conjunction with Con Edison, "Fact Sheet."
138. YMPJ encouraged community residents and workers to attend meetings designed to inform the public of plans to clean up the site. I attended one of them in 2003.
139. David Shuffler, interview with author, December 17, 2010. The previous quotation is from YMPJ's website at www.ympj.org/about.html (accessed March 26, 2011).
140. Shoelace Master Plan, "Recommendations: Vegetation Management & Restoration," http://66.240.202.37/puma/images/usersubmitted/file/Shoelace%20Master%20Plan%20Recommend%20-%20C.pdf (accessed March 3, 2011). The entire Shoelace Park Master Plan is best accessed through http://www.bronxriver.org/?pg=content&p=aboutus&m1=1&m2=3&m3=81, February 2010 (accessed March 3, 2011).
141. For brief descriptions of notable locations in the Westchester section of the river, go to Friends of Westchester Parks, http://www.friendsofwestchesterparks.com/BronxRiverAudioTour.html. For a

brochure go to http://www.friendsofwestchesterparks.com/images/PDFS/BronxRiverWalkBrochure.pdf. Information about Garrett Park Neighborhood Association is from Hank Stroobants, personal interviews, February 24, 2011, and March 29, 2011, and David DeLucia, telephone interview November 30, 2010.

142. Alexie Torres-Fleming, quoted in Amy Frykholm, "Justice for the South Bronx: activist Alexie Torres-Fleming," Bnet, July 28, 2009, http://findarticles.com/p/articles/mi_m1058/is_15_126/ai_n35579548/pg_2/?tag=content;col1 (accessed March 31, 2010). The park that opened "last month" was Concrete Plant Park between Westchester Avenue and Bruckner Boulevard. Starlight Park is expected to reopen in 2012. Table 5 contains updated car and tire removal statistics that have been inserted into this quotation.

143. The date of the zoning application is reported in "Active Land Use Application Filed with the Department of City Planning as of 04/08/11," http://www.nyc.gov/html/dcp/pdf/lu_apps/ulurp_x06.pdf; Joan Byron, letter to Robert Dobruskin, director of the Environmental Assessment and Review Division, New York City Department of City Planning, Bronx River Alliance, March 15, 2010. Joan Byron was the third board chair of the Bronx River Alliance. As this book goes to press, Kellie Terry-Sepulveda has taken over as the chair of the alliance.

8. Reclaiming a Natural Resource

144. Bronx River Alliance, "Ecological Restoration and Management Plan," http://www.Bronxriver.org/plans, 2006; "Bronx River Watershed Assessment and Management Plan," White Plains: Westchester County Department of Planning, 2007; Center for Watershed Protection, "Bronx River Intermunicipal Watershed Management Plan," 2011. Worth noting is the intermunicipal report has a watershed-wide focus from the Kensico Dam to the East River.

145. Bronx River Alliance, "Ecological Restoration and Management Plan," Appendix A. Just preceding this quotation, a technical statement tells us there is a continuing discharge of "fecal coliform

bacteria into the Bronx River during dry weather. Fecal coliform levels ranged from 800 mpn (most probable number) to 16,000,000 mpn per 100 milliliters (mL), exceeding the water quality standard of 200 fecal coliforms (mpn) per 100 mL by orders of magnitude. In 1999, a study conducted by the New York State Department of Environmental Conservation in Westchester County revealed discharge levels that varied between 2 mpn/100mL to as high as 308,500 mpn/100 mL and contamination in the Bronx River that ranged from 230 to 54,000 mpn/100 mL."

146. Bronx River Alliance, "Ecological Restoration and Management Plan," chapter 3, section 2.

147. SWIM, "Mission and Platform," http://swimmablenyc.info/?page_id=4 (accessed April 9, 2010).

148. The Clean Water Act of 1972, an important milestone toward the improvement of the nation's waterways, was necessary but not sufficient to accomplish the task. The work of environmental improvement in the Bronx River Watershed by numerous community organizations was and is necessary. The Clean Water Act, along with the Clean Air Act of 1970 and the National Environmental Policy Act of 1969 and the associated government funding and regulation of the environment, only mark the beginning of an important increase in the nation's environmental consciousness.

149. Linda Cox, interview with author, November 18, 2010.

150. Ibid.

151. Dart Westphal, e-mail, December 10, 2010.

152. Bronx River Alliance, Annual Report, 2004, http://bronxriver.org/puma/images/usersubmitted/file/2004AnnualReport.pdf (accessed May 2, 2011).

153. Center for Watershed Protection, "Bronx River Intermunicipal Watershed Management Plan," i.

154. Green job workers contribute to building a green infrastructure with the focus of preserving or restoring environmental quality. Members of the Conservation Crew, installers of roof gardens (green roofs), contractors who increase a home's environmental efficiency by, for example, increasing its insulation all have green jobs.

155. The headquarters are located at the New York Department of Parks and Recreation, 1 Bronx River Parkway, Bronx, New York, November 20, 2009.

156. Linda Cox, personal interview, November 18, 2010.

EPILOGUE

157. This is a composite description of the annual Amazing Bronx River Flotilla, starting in 1999 then organized jointly by Partnerships for Parks and the Bronx River Working Group. On May 1, 2010, 177 people went down the river in sixty-nine canoes and nineteen kayaks. That year, because of funding cutbacks, there were no T-shirts. Signup for future Amazing Bronx River Flotillas will be available on the BronxRiver.org website about a month before the event but becomes fully subscribed within a few hours after it is posted. For me, these canoe trips down the Bronx River are one of the highlights of my participation with the Bronx River Alliance in that they are a hopeful statement about the environmental future, not only of the Bronx River but of the broader environment as well.

ACKNOWLEDGEMENTS

158. For my transcript of his presentation, see Ultan, "History of the Bronx River."

Bibliography

Aqua Explorers, Inc./Shipwreck Expo. "The Bronx Queen Shipwreck: New York and New Jersey's (Wreck Valley)," http://www.aquaexplorers.com/bronx.htm (accessed November 12, 2010).

Barlow, Elizabeth. "New York: A Once and Future Arcadia." *New York Magazine* (November 29, 1971).

Bolton, Henry B. Obituary. *New York Times*, December 20, 1895.

Bolton, Reginald Pelham. *Indian Life of Long Ago in the City of New York*. New York: Harmony, 1972.

Bolton, Robert, Jr. *History of the County of Westchester from Its First Settlement to the Present Time*. 2 vols. New York: Alexander and Gould, 1848.

Bracker, Milton. "Bronx River's Trout Scorn City's 'Incomplete' Anglers: Motley Throngs Match Wits With 560 Fish, Which Come Off Much the Better—They Snub All Lures, Even Curtain Rod." *New York Times*, April 7, 1935.

Burrows, Edwin G., and Mike Wallace. *Gotham: A History of New York City to 1898*. New York: Oxford, 1999.

Cantwell, Anne-Marie, and Diana diZerega Wall. *Unearthing Gotham*. New Haven, CT, and London: Yale University, 2001.

Carison, Catherine C. "History Through a Pinhole: The [In]Significance of Atlantic Salmon," *Common Ground* 8, nos. 3 and 4 (Fall/Winter 1996).

Caro, Robert A. *The Power Broker: Robert Moses and the Fall of New York*. New York: Vintage Books, 1975.

Cronon, William. *Changes in the Land: Indians, Colonists, and the Ecology of New England*. New York: Hill and Wang, 2003.

Cumbler, John T. *Reasonable Use: The People, the Environment, and the State, New England 1790–1930*. New York: Oxford University, 2001.

de Kadt, Maarten. "The Bronx River: A Classroom for Environmental, Political and Historical Studies." *Capitalism Nature Socialism* (June 2006).

Diamond, Jared. *Collapse: How Societies Choose to Fail Or Succeed*. New York: Viking, 2005.

Dunlap, David W. "From Tobacco Leaves to Wedding Bouquets, 169 Years in the Bronx," *New York Times*, February 8, 2009.

Galusha, Diane. *Liquid Assets: A History of New York City's Water System*. Fleishmanns, NY: Purple Mountain, 1999.

Goldman, Joanne Abel. *Building New York's Sewers: Developing Mechanisms of Urban Management*. West Lafayette, IN: Purdue University Press, 1997.

Gonzalez, Evelyn. *The Bronx*. New York: Columbia University Press, 2004.

Grassi, Carrie. "The Development of the Bronx River Alliance, Lessons in Organizational Structure and Goal Implementation," Urban Nature and City Design, MIT, http://ocw.mit.edu/ans7870/11/11.308/f05/assignments/cgrassi/index.htm (accessed March 27, 2010).

Greenburgh Nature Center and Scarsdale Historical Society. *Bronx River Retrospective: 300 Years of Life along the Bronx River Valley*. White Plains, NY: Greenburgh Nature Center and the Scarsdale Historical Society, 1983.

Hermalyn, Gary. "A History of the Bronx River." *Bronx County Historical Society Journal* 19 (Spring 1982): 1–22.

Ishiguri, Keiji. "Secrets Behind the Stone: The History of Tuckahoe's Old Stone Mill, Revealed!" Unpublished manuscript, 2002. New York State Archives Research Award, Tuckahoe Historical Society.

Jackson, Kenneth T. *Crabgrass Frontier: The Suburbanization of the United States*, New York: Oxford University, 1985.

Jenkins, Stephen. *The Story of the Bronx: From the Purchase Made by the Dutch from the Indians in 1639 to the Present Day*. New York: Putnam, 1912.

Jonnes, Jill. *South Bronx Rising: The Rise, Fall, and Resurrection of an American City*. New York: Fordham University Press, 2002.

MacDonald, Barbara Shay. "The Bronx River: Boundary of Indian Tribes, Colonies, Manors, Cities and Villages," http://www.scarsdalehistory.org/PDFs/BronxRiver.htm.

Mahler, Jonathan. *The Bronx Is Burning: 1977, Baseball, Politics, and the Battle for the Soul of a City*. New York: Picador, 2007.

Mann, Charles C. *1491: New Revelations of the Americas Before Columbus*, New York: Alfred A. Knopf, 2005.

Merchant, Carolyn. *Ecological Revolutions: Nature, Gender, and Science in New England*, Chapel Hill: University of North Carolina, 1989.

Miller, Benjamin. *Fat of the Land: Garbage of New York The Last Two Hundred Years.* New York: Four Walls Eight Windows, 2000.

Panayotakis, Costas. "Capitalism, Socialism, and Economic Democracy: Reflections on Today's Crisis and Tomorrow's Possibilities." *Capitalism Nature Socialism* (December 2010).

Rachlin, Joe W. "Notes on the Dams of the Bronx River," *History of the Bronx Borough: City of New York*, New York: North Side Press, 1906.

Sanderson, Eric W. *Mannahatta: A Natural History of New York City*. New York: Abrams, 2009.

Sanderson, Eric W., and Danielle T. LaBruna. "Mapping the Historical Ecology and Reconstructing the Historical Flora of the Lower Bronx River: A Guide for Ecosystem Restoration and Outreach." Wildlife Conservation Society, 2005.

Smith, Dennis. *Report from Engine Co. 82*. New York: McCall, 1972.

Steinberg, Theodore. *Nature Incorporated: Industrialization and the Waters of New England*, Amherst: University of Massachusetts, 1991.

Stewart, Barbara. "In Bronx, A Plan for Reeling in Fish, Not Cars." *New York Times*, November 20, 1999.

———. "A River Rises." *New York Times*, December 3, 2000.

Ultan, Lloyd. "Jonas Bronck and the First Settlement of the Bronx." *Bronx County Historical Society Journal* 16, no. 2 (1989): 53–67.

———. *The Northern Borough: A History of the Bronx*. New York: Bronx County Historical Society, 2009.

Ultan, Lloyd, and Gary Hermalyn. *The Birth of the Bronx, 1606–1900.* New York: Bronx County Historical Society, 2000.

OTHER RESOURCES

Bronx River Restoration. *Master Plan.* Bronx, NY: Bronx River Restoration, 1980. Copy in possession of the author given to him by Dart Westphal.

Bruner Foundation, Inc. "2009 Rudy Bruner Award: Silver Medal Winner: Hunts Point Riverside Park." Bronx, http://www.brunerfoundation.org/rba/pdfs/2009/Hunts%20Point.FINAL.pdf (accessed March 2, 2011).

Center for Watershed Protection. "Bronx River Intermunicipal Watershed Management Plan: Working Together for Our River," Ellicott City, MD: Center for Watershed Protection, 2011.

Friends of Westchester Parks. Audio/visual tour of the Bronx River, http://www.friendsofwestchesterparks.com/BronxRiverAudioTour.html.

Insurance Maps of the City of New York. Vol. 12. New York: Perris & Browne, 1882. Collection of the New York Historical Society.

Master Plan for Shoelace Park on the Bronx River Greenway. February 2010. http://66.240.202.37/puma/images/usersubmitted/file/Shoelace%20Master%20Plan%20Recommend%20-%20C.pdf (accessed March 3, 2011).

New York City Department of Environmental Protection. "Bronx River Waterbody/Watershed Facility Plan Report." New York: July 2009.

New York Times. "Calls Nearby Rivers Mere Open Sewers," March 7, 1910.

———. "Filthy State of the Bronx River," December 7, 1881.

North Side Board of Trade. *The Great North Side of Borough of the Bronx.* N.p.: 1897.

Report of the Bronx Parkway Commission. N.p.: 1918. http://books.google.com/books?id=Y47NAAAAMAAJ&printsec=frontcover&dq=inauthor:%22New+York+(State).+Bronx+Parkway+Commission%22&hl=en&ei=48DfTZPXIIHhiAKU4JHvCg&sa=X&oi=book_result&ct=result&resnum=1&ved=0CC4Q6AEwAA#v=onepage&q&f=false.

Report of the Bronx Valley Sewer Commission, Organized under Chapter 1021, Laws of 1895, 1896. Westchester County Archives.

Ultan, Lloyd. "History of the Bronx River." Presentation at Fannie Lou Hamer Freedom High School, November 5, 2002, http://bronxriver.org/?pg=content&p=abouttheriver&m1=9&m2=58.

Westchester.gov. "Databook Westchester County," November 2005. http://www.westchestergov.com/Planning/research/Databook/Data%20Book200515.pdf (accessed March 12, 2010).

Weston, William, Esq. "On the Practicability of Introducing WATER of the River Bronx into This City." Report to common council, March 16, 1799. Westchester Archives, New York Public Library.

INTERVIEWS

Carter, Majora. October 25, 2010, and multiple dates.

Cob, Ken (New York City Municipal Archives). May, 2010.

Cox, Linda. November 18, 2010.

DeLucia, David (director of park facilities, Westchester County). November 30, 2010, and April 5, 2011.

DeVillo, Stephen (Bronx River Alliance). Multiple dates.

DiNapoli, Louie. August 27, 2010.

Donovan, Dan (Bronx Borough President's Map Office). November 23, 2009.

Griffin, Damian (Bronx River Alliance). February 23, 2011, and multiple dates.

Miller, Joyce. March 15, 2010.

Raskin, Jack. April 10, 2010.

Shuffler, David. December 17, 2010.

Stroobants, Hank. February 24, 2011, and March 29, 2011.

Westphal, Dart. Multiple dates.

White, Philip A. (former mayor of Tuckahoe), and his staff. October 6, 2010.

Yalowitz, Nat. March 16, 2010.

Index

A

Amazing Bronx River Flotilla 26, 99, 116, 144
Amtrak 46, 94
Anderberg, Ruth 70, 98
Appalachian Mountain Club 74
Aquehung 15, 16, 17, 18, 19, 23, 131

B

Badaracco, Bart 59
Bathgate, James 37
Battle of White Plains 25
Bloomberg, Michael R. 95
Bolton Dam 38, 40, 74
Bolton, Henry B. 38
Broad Street Sewer 56
Broadway Sewer 57
Bronck, Jonas 13, 20, 21, 22, 131
Bronck, Peter 21, 22
Broncksland 23
Bronk. *See* Bronck, Jonas
Bronx Bleachery. *See* Bolton Dam
Bronx Company. *See* Bolton Dam
Bronx Courthouse 63
Bronxdale 38, 39
Bronx International Exposition 66
Bronx Park 21, 27, 33, 38, 54, 58, 65, 66, 132, 134
Bronx Parkway Commission 58, 59, 60, 103
Bronx Queen 87, 88, 89, 92, 141
Bronx River Alliance 7, 71, 72, 73, 75, 76, 78, 79, 82, 84, 87, 95, 98, 99, 100, 101, 103, 106, 109, 111, 113, 114, 144
Bronx River Art Center 115
Bronx River Greenway 98, 103, 111
Bronx River Paint Company 37, 134
Bronx River Parkway 9, 58, 59, 60, 62, 63, 65, 66, 67, 100, 101, 117, 138, 144
Bronx River Parkway Reservation Conservancy 100
Bronx River Restoration 10, 70, 71, 75, 77, 98, 101, 140

Bronx River Working Group (BRWG) 71, 72, 73, 75, 76, 77, 84, 87, 117, 144
Bronx Valley Sewer Commission 52, 53
Bronxville, New York 41, 48, 52, 58, 65, 101
Bronx Zoo 38, 40, 41, 54, 74, 115, 134
Brooklyn Board of Sewer Commissioners 57
Brooklyn, New York 25
Bruckner Boulevard 62
Burr, Aaron 25, 28
Burroughs-Wellcome Pharmaceuticals 34
Byron, Joan 142

C

Campbell, Robert 48
Canal Street Sewer 56
Caro, Robert A. 10
Carpenter, Elizabeth Ann 33
Carrión, Adolfo, Jr. 141
Carter, Majora 72, 73, 86, 117
Chandler, A.C. 39
Chase Bank 27
Clason's Point 15, 16
combined sewer overflow (CSO). *See* combined storm water and sewer system
combined storm water and sewer system 53, 56, 57, 62, 70, 101, 107, 108
Concrete Plant Park 46, 76, 81, 88, 91, 92, 94, 95
Con Edison 7, 42, 113
Connecticut River 15, 23
Conservation Crew 80, 88, 99, 100, 111, 115, 116, 143
Cox, Linda 80, 113, 114, 140
Coxsackie, New York 21
Crawford's Saw Mill 40, 41
Crestwood, New York 58
Cross County Parkway 65
Croton Reservoir 49, 56
Croton River 28
Croton Water Filtration Plant 95

D

Davis Brook 15
DeLancey, James 25
DeLancey, Peter 25
Diaz, Ruben, Jr. 117, 141
Drew Gardens 115
Dunwoodie Substation 7, 113
Dutch 20, 21, 22, 23, 56, 98
Dutch West India Company 20

E

Eastchester 48
Eastchester Manufacturing Company 33
East River 10, 16, 25, 48, 50, 52, 57, 70, 71, 75, 107, 129, 142
East Tremont 10, 107, 139

F

Fannie Lou Hamer Freedom High School 10, 115, 140
fecal coliform 106, 143
French Charlie's 54

G

Garrett Park Neighborhood Association (GPNA) 100
Garth Wood 101
Gilbert, Cass 45, 46
Golden Ball 74, 75
Grassy Sprain Brook 9
Green, Andrew Haswell 48
Green County Historical Society Museum 22

green job training 111, 143
Gun Hill 25

H

Haddon, Thomas 23
Halloran, Edward J. 140
Harlem, New York 21
Harlem River 15, 129, 132
Hartsdale, New York 41, 58, 101
Haubold's Gunpowder Mill 41
Hodgman Rubber Company 34
Hoffner, Jenny 72, 73, 117
Home Owners' Loan Corporation (HOLC) 64, 65
Horton's Tannery Mill 41
Hudson, Henry 20
Hudson River 15, 17, 21, 56, 129
Hudson River Estuary 55
Hudson Valley 17
Hunts Point 15, 87
Hunts Point Food Market 84, 86, 87
Hunts Point Riverside Park 86, 87
Hunts Point Water Treatment Plant 57, 67
Hutchinson, Anne 21
Hutchinson River 15, 24, 129
Hutchinson River Parkway 21, 65

I

Indians 15, 20, 23. *See* Native Americans
Interstate Highway Act of 1956 68

K

Kensico Dam 50, 51, 71, 75
Kensico Reservoir 41, 49, 56, 134
Kieft's War 23
Kingsbridge 49

L

Lillian and Amy Goldman Stone Mill. *See* Lorillard Snuff Mill
Long Island Sound 110
Lorillard Dam 32
Lorillard, George 37
Lorillard, Peter 37
Lorillard, Pierre 31
Lorillard Snuff Mill 31, 32, 34
Lorillard Tobacco Company 31
Lydig, David 37
Lydig, Phillip 27

M

Manhattan 17, 20, 25, 27, 45, 56
Manhattan Company 27, 28
manufactured gas plant (MGP) 42, 95
Massachusetts 23, 33, 39
Master Plan, 1980 70, 71, 75, 110
Memer, Peter A. 37
Merrimack River, Massachusetts 23
Miller, Joyce 67
Morrisania 21, 48, 49, 65
Moses, Robert 67, 100
Mosholu Preservation Corporation 73
Mount Vernon, New York 48, 52, 58

N

National Park Service 74
Native Americans 18, 19
- Lenape 17, 20, 130
- Manhattans 15
- Mannahatta 17
- Mohegans 15
- Siwanoys 15
- Wappinger Confederation 17
- Weckquaesgeeks 15

New England 15, 17, 23, 33, 131
New Hampshire 23
New York and Harlem Railroad 45
New York Botanical Garden 31, 32, 33, 54, 62, 68, 115
New York City Department of City Planning 103
New York City Department of Environmental Protection 107
New York City Department of Parks and Recreation 74, 78, 79, 81, 85, 86, 87, 91, 95, 99, 140, 144
New York City Parks Foundation 74
New York City Partnership for Parks 74, 84
New York National Guard 93, 94
New York, New Haven & Hartford Railroad 45, 94
New York State Conservation Commission 66
New York State Department of Environmental Conservation (DEC) 7, 113
New York State Department of Transportation 87
New York State Office of Parks, Recreation and Historic Preservation 95
New York Stock Market 27
Nieuw Amsterdam 20, 22
Nieuw Netherland 21, 23
Northern Annex 50, 57
Northern Union Gas Company. *See* manufactured gas plant

O

Old Stone Mill, Tuckahoe, New York 33, 34, 35, 36, 41
174th Street Bridge 67, 88, 95, 97, 115

P

Passaic River, New Jersey 52
Pataki, George 117
Pawtucket, Rhode Island 33
P. Lorillard Company. *See* Lorillard Tobacco Company
Point Community Development Corporation (the Point) 72, 73, 86, 111

R

Raskin, Jack 66, 67
red lining 65
Revolutionary War 25
Rhode Island 23
Richardson/DeLancey/Lydig Mill Dam 25, 26, 116
Richardson, William 25
Riverdale 65
Rocking the Boat 86, 111

S

Saw Mill River 15, 24, 52, 65
Scarsdale Dam 101
Scarsdale, New York 40, 58, 101, 134
Serrano, José E. 95, 117
sewershed 56
Sheridan Expressway 43, 95
Shoelace Park 65, 99, 115
Shuffler, David 88, 95, 96, 97
Sound View 65
Sprain Brook 9, 15
Spuyten Duyvill 57
Stamford, Connecticut 15
Starlight Park 43, 88, 95, 98, 115, 117, 139
Starlight Park Amusement Park 66
Stern, Henry J. 117, 139
Stone Mill, Tuckahoe, New York 36

Storm Water Infrastructure Matters (SWIM) 108
storm water management 99, 103, 108, 112
Sustainable South Bronx 86, 111, 117
Swain's Cutlery Mill 41

T

Taconic Parkway 65
Tait, William J. 33
Terry-Sepulveda, Kellie 142
Throckmorton, John 23
Throggs Neck 23
Tibbetts Brook 15, 132
Tippett, George 132
Tippetts Brook. *See* Tibbetts Brook
Torres-Fleming, Alexie 73, 102, 110, 117
Transit-Mix Concrete 89, 90, 140
Tuckahoe Cotton Factory 33
Tuckahoe, New York 33, 41, 52, 58, 117
23rd and 24th Wards 46, 54, 57

U

Ultan, Lloyd 64

V

Valhalla, New York 9, 10, 50, 58
Van Cortlandt, Jacobus 24
Van Cortlandt Lake 24
Van Cortlandt Park 132
Village of Kensico 50
Vosburgh, Herman 37

W

Ward's Island Sewage Plant 57
Washington, George 25
Westchester Light Horse 25
Westchester Square 98
West Farms 38, 40, 49, 70, 87, 103, 106
West Farms Square, The Bronx 66
Weston, William 27
Westphal, Dart 73
White Plains, New York 25, 41, 45, 52, 58, 134
Whitney, Eli 33
Williamsbridge 52
Willis, Edward 48
Woodlawn 52, 55, 61
Woodlawn Cemetery 25
Woonasquetucket River, Rhode Island 23, 33
Wright Mills, Ruben and Thomas 41

Y

Yalowitz, Nat 66, 67
Yankee Stadium 63
Yonkers, New York 7, 24, 55, 59, 65, 100, 106
Youth Ministries for Peace and Justice (YMPJ) 73, 87, 88, 95, 96, 97, 110, 117

About the Author

Photo by Karen Smith.

Maarten de Kadt has a doctorate in economics. His examination of the environment over the past twenty years exemplifies his desire to improve the lives of others. He has studied problems associated with municipal solid waste management, the delivery of drinking water and the removal and treatment of sewage waste. As a high school teacher, he was introduced to a destroyed but recovering Bronx River and used it to help students understand the possibilities of environmental recovery and of personal empowerment. Dr. de Kadt continues to be an environmental and community activist. He is a member of the Bronx River Alliance's Board of Directors and of the Bronx Borough President's Solid Waste Management Advisory Board.

9 780979 168543